Islamic Geo
Patterns

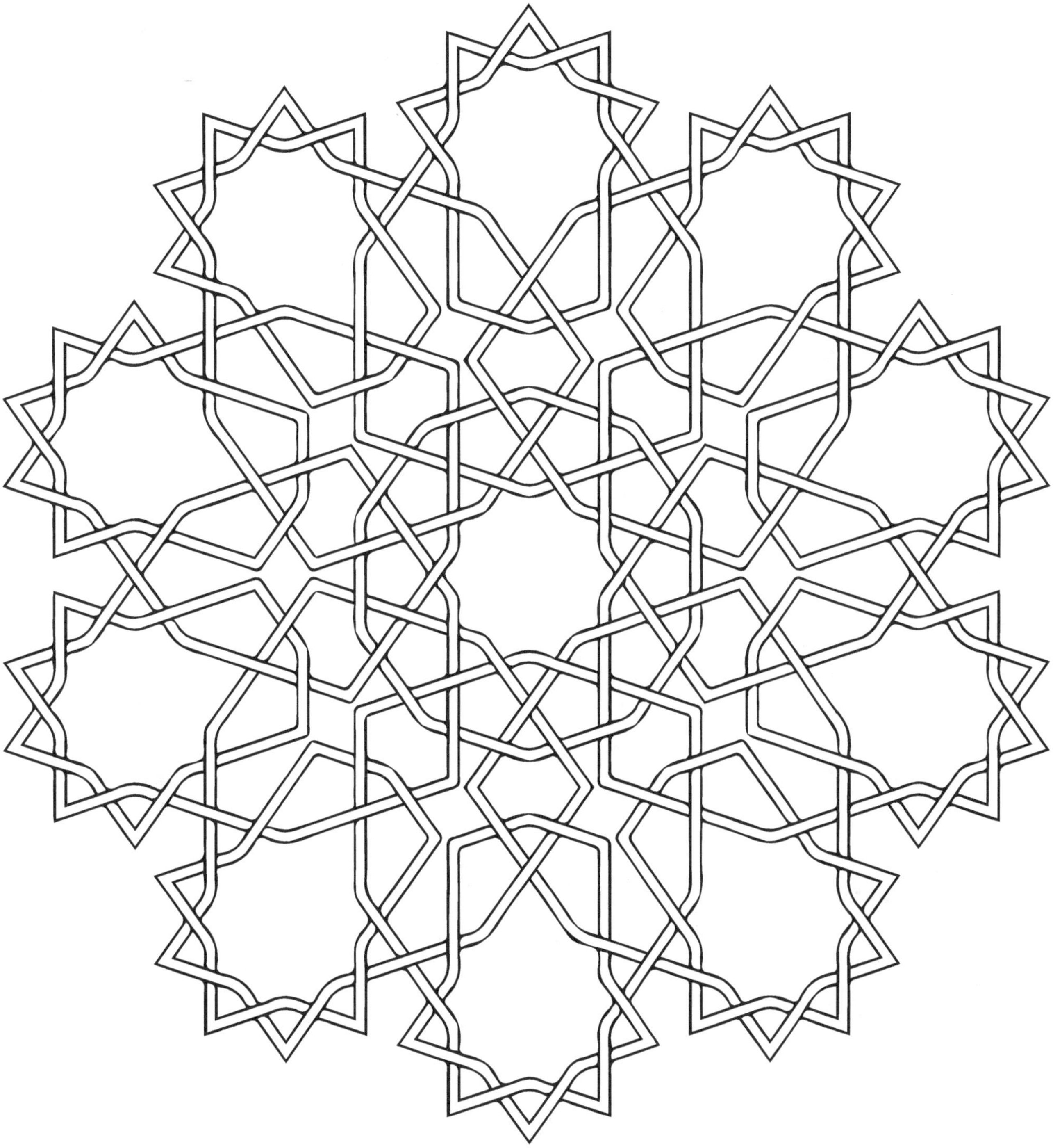

This Book Belongs To

____

Color Test Page

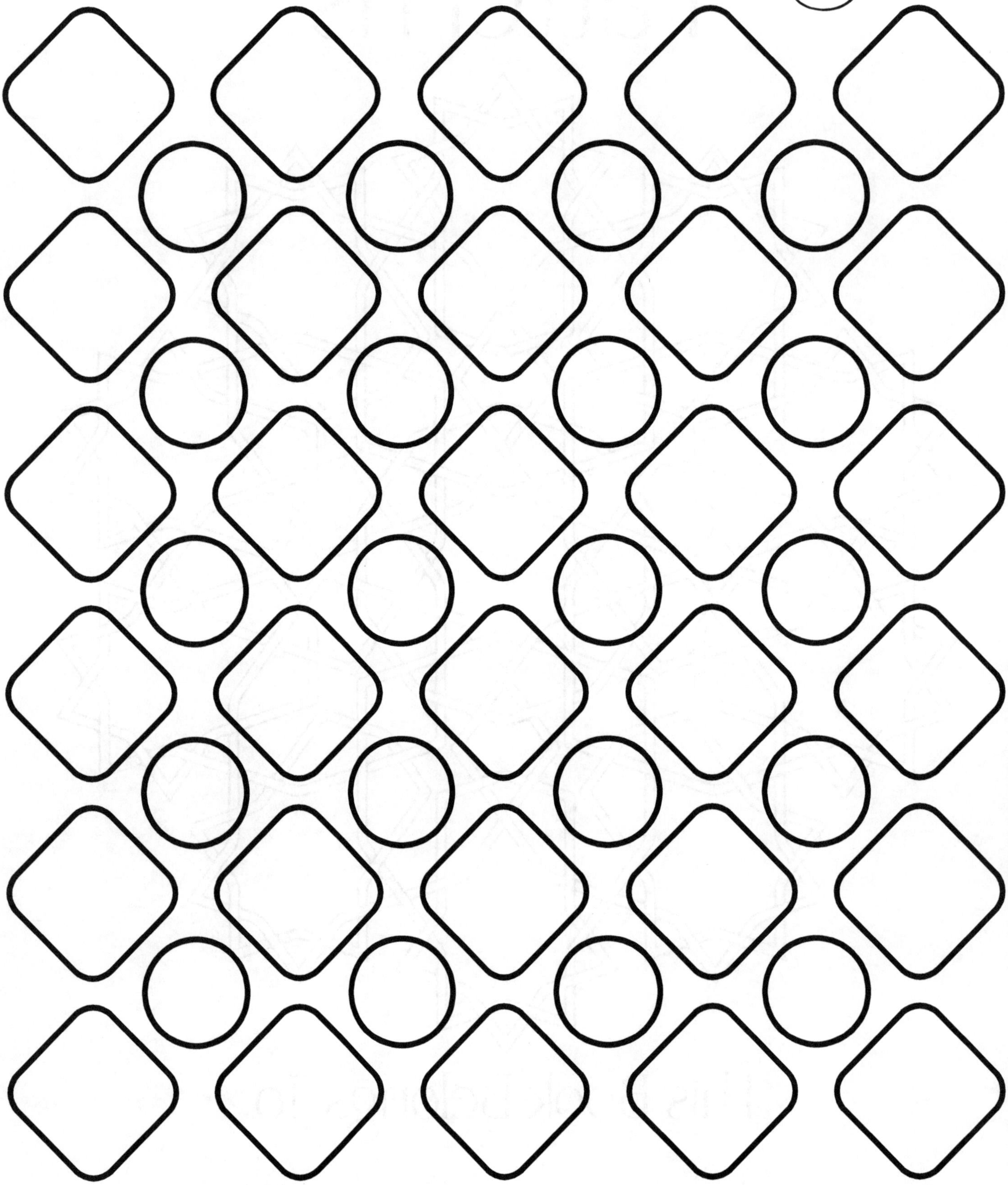

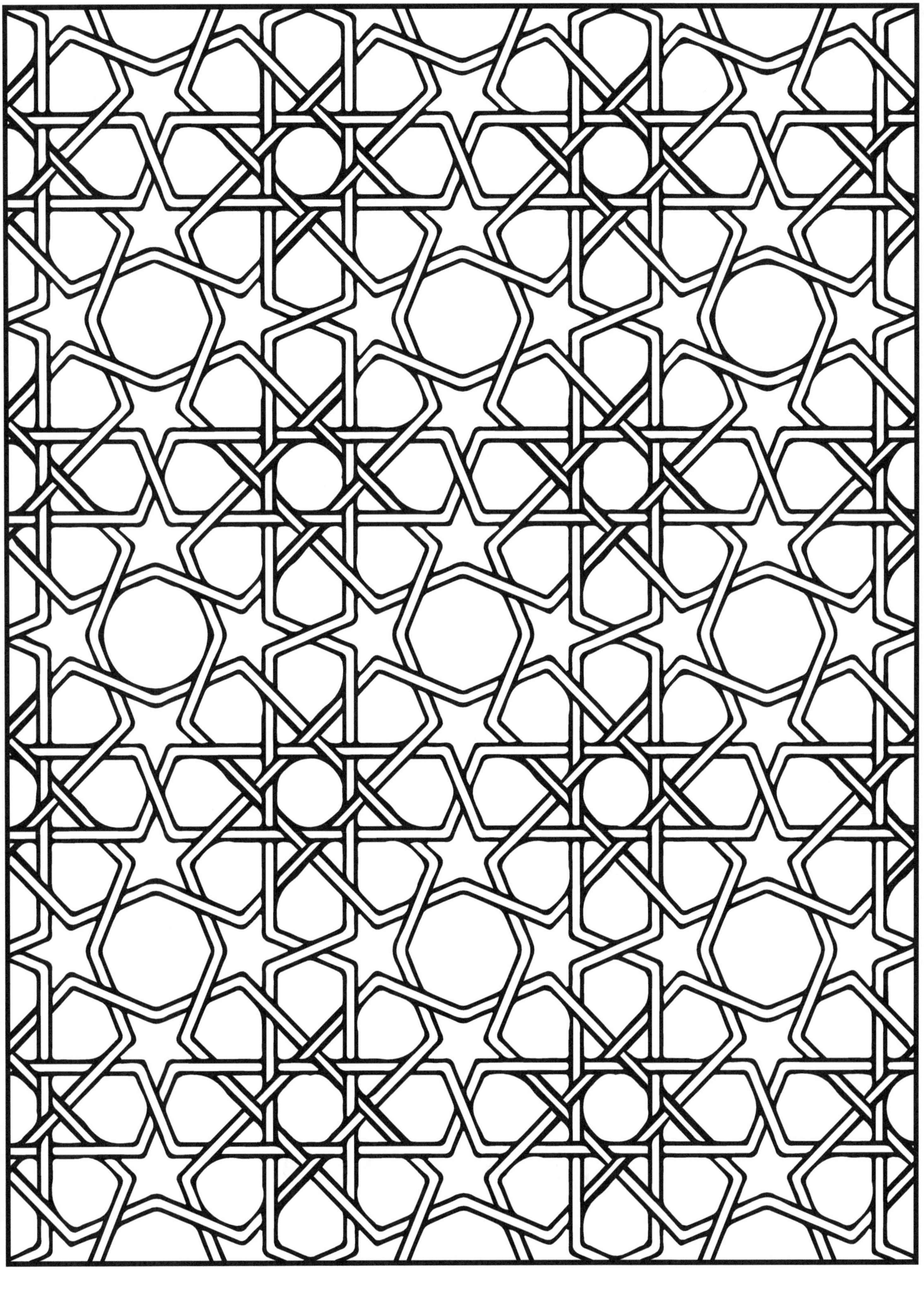

STAY RELAXED

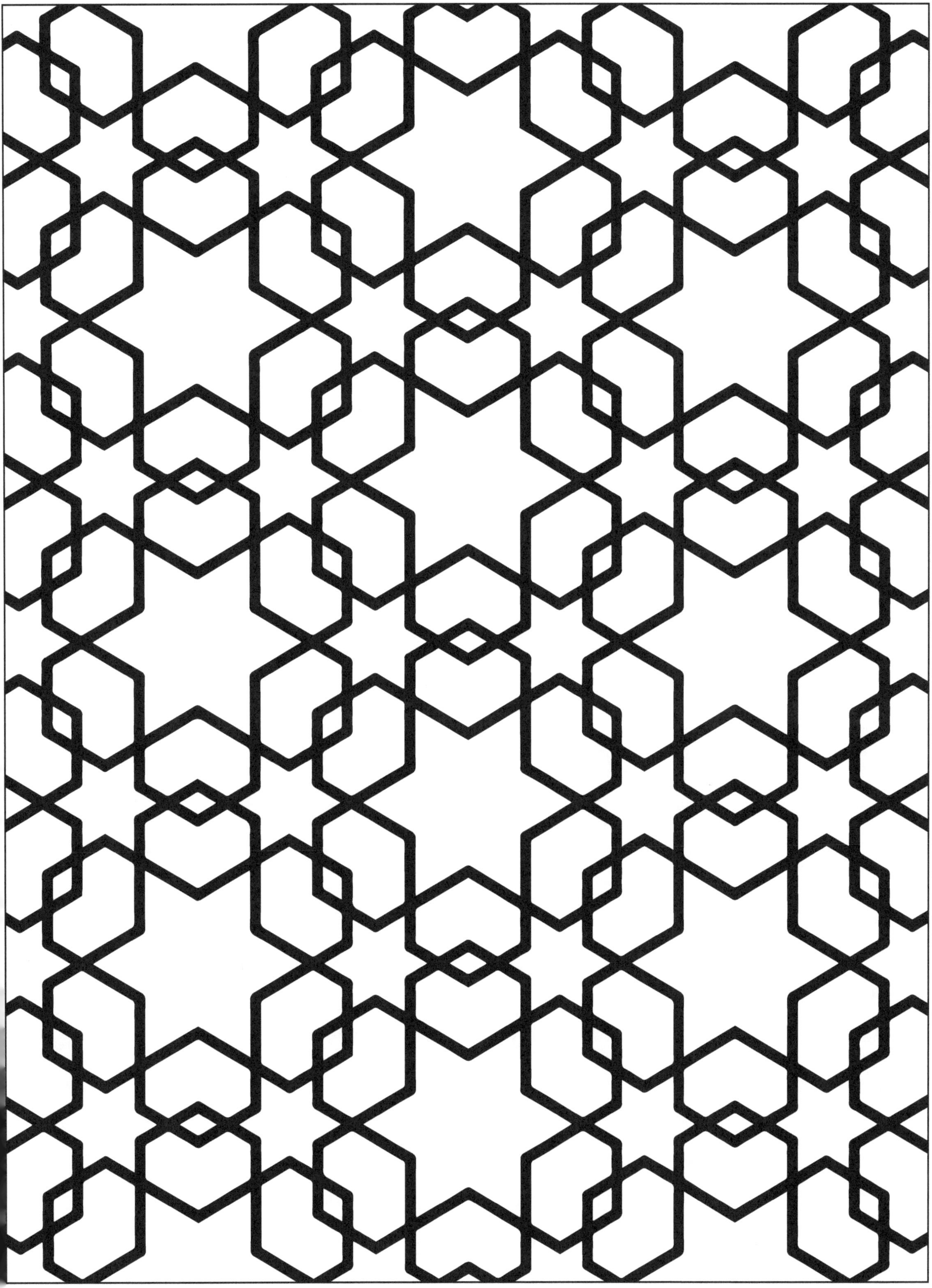

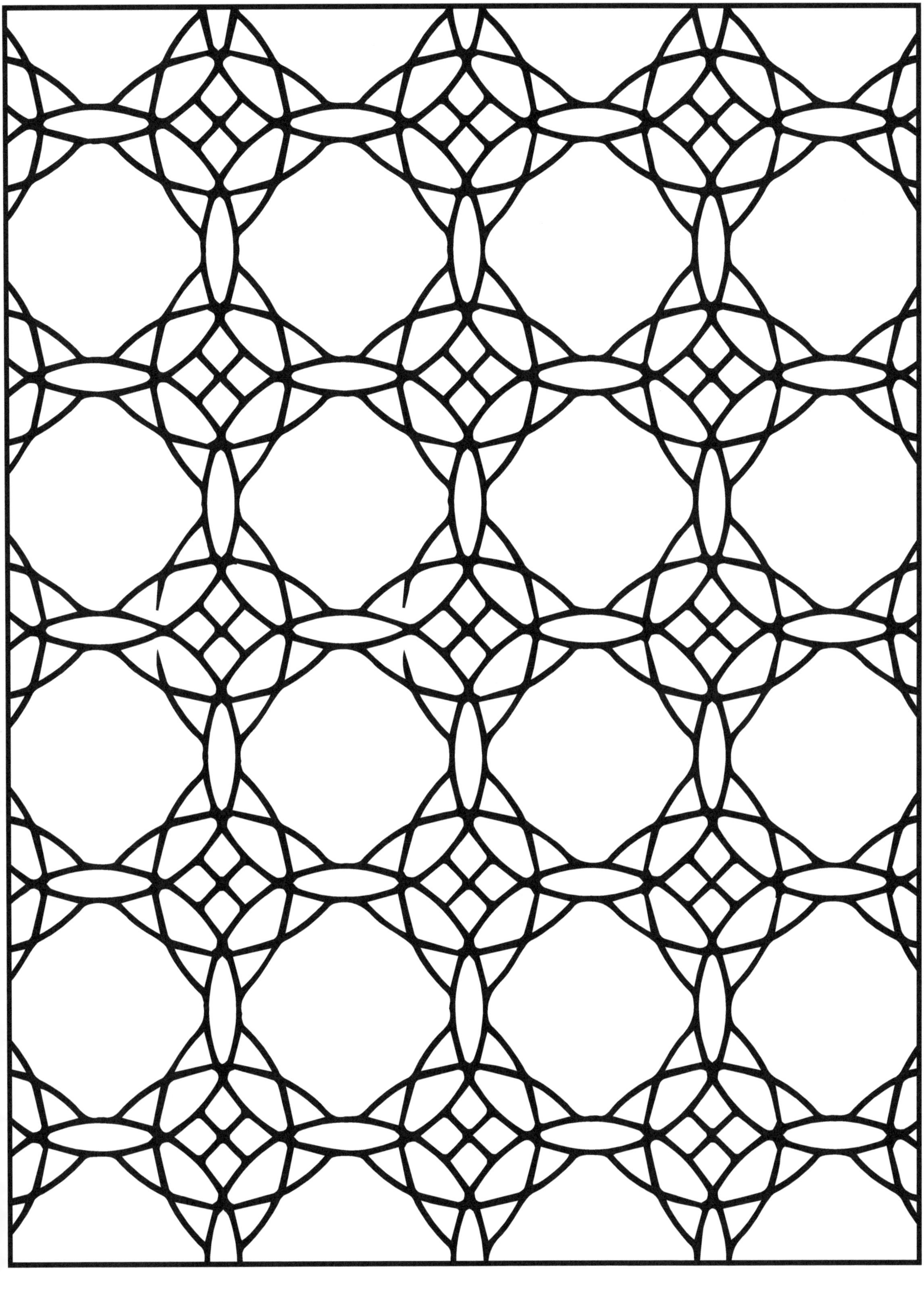

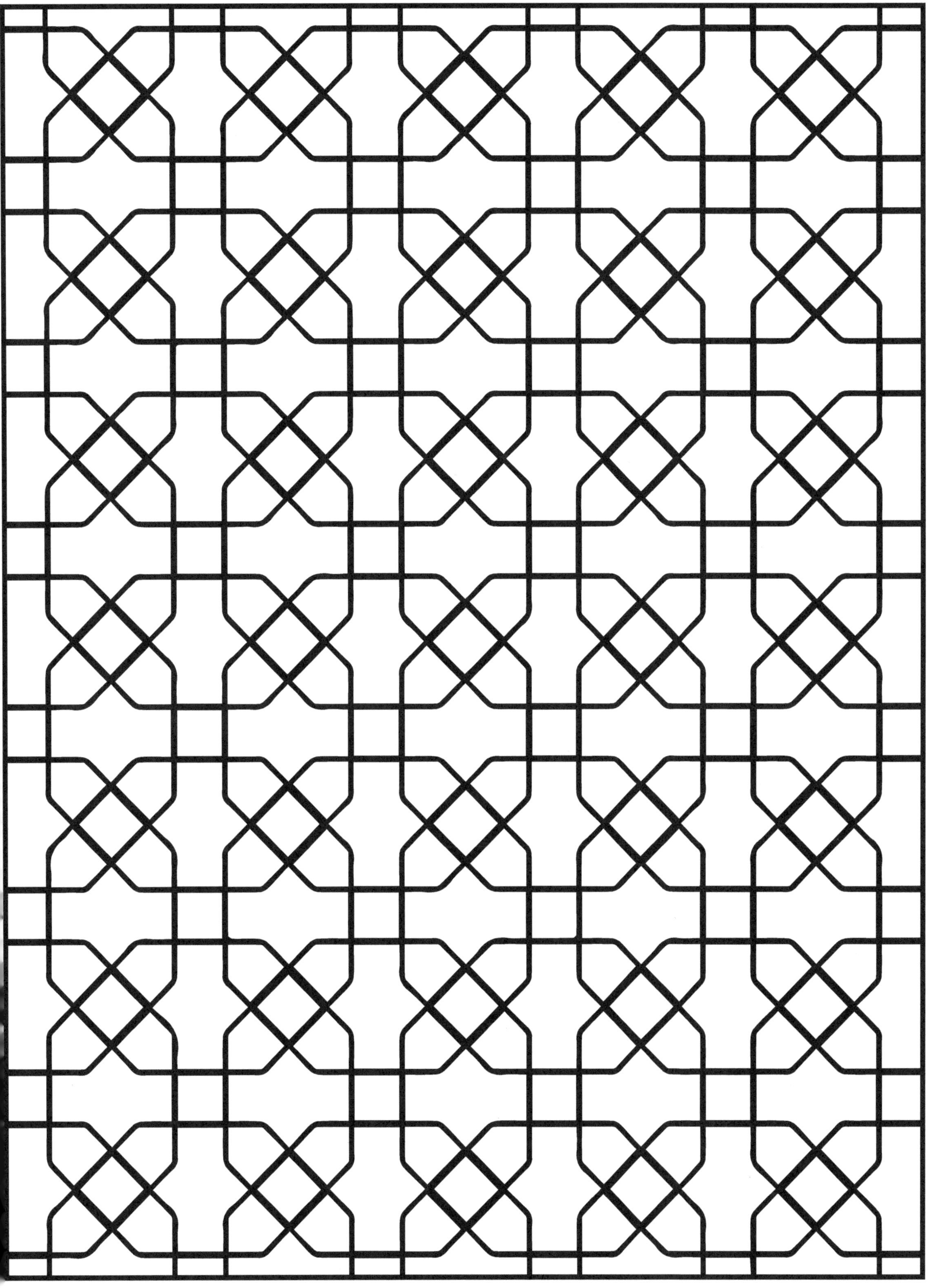

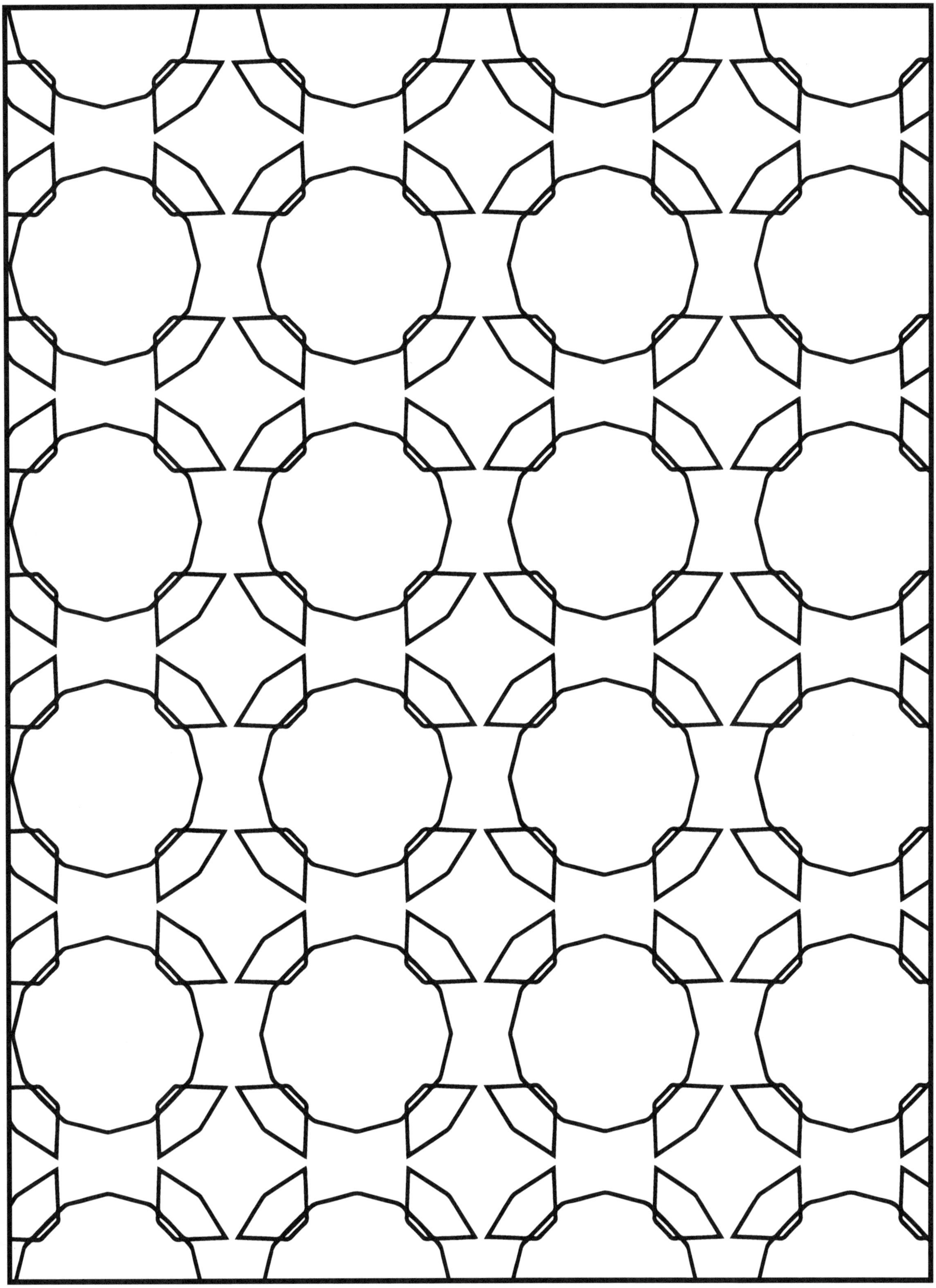

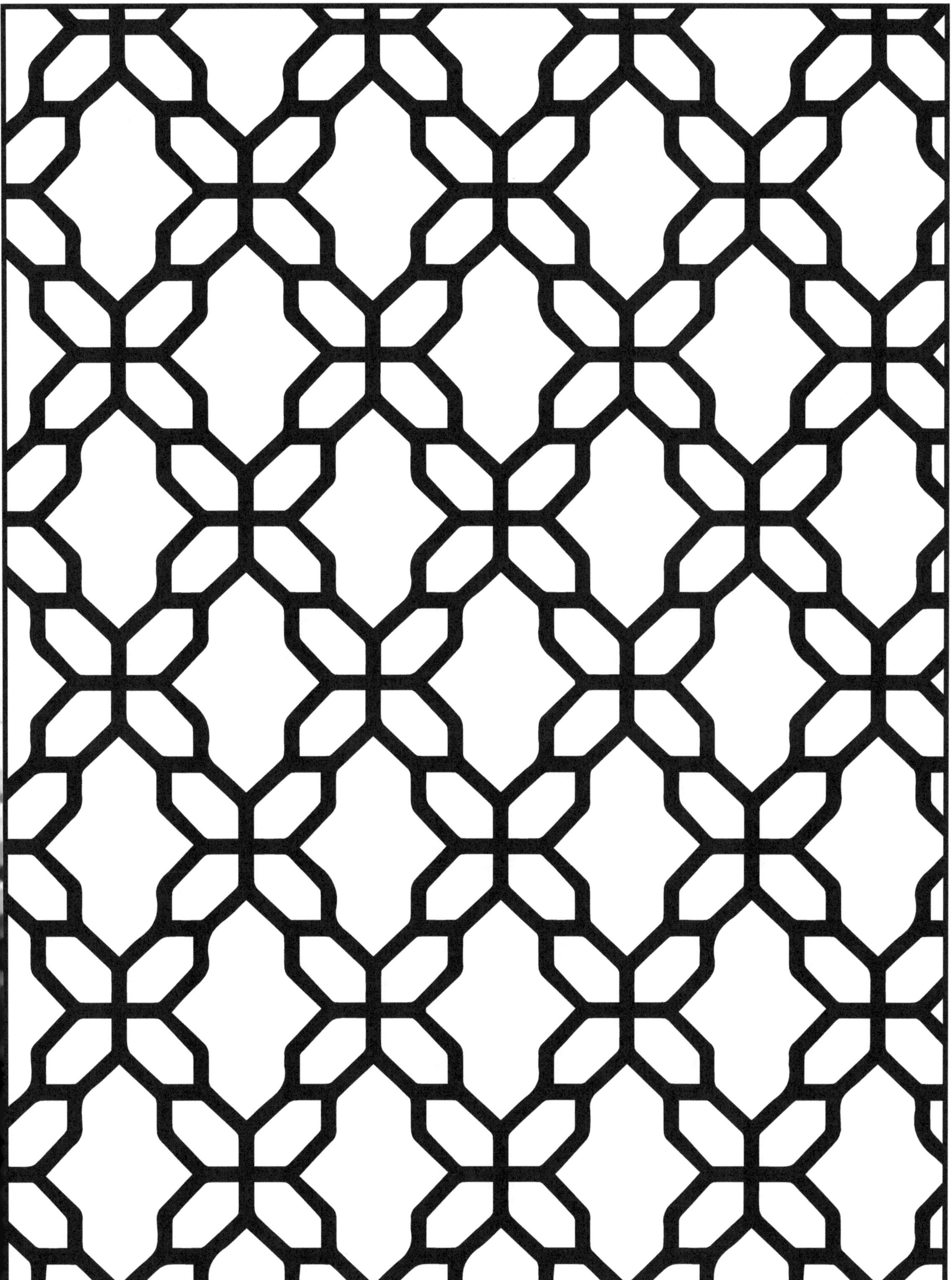

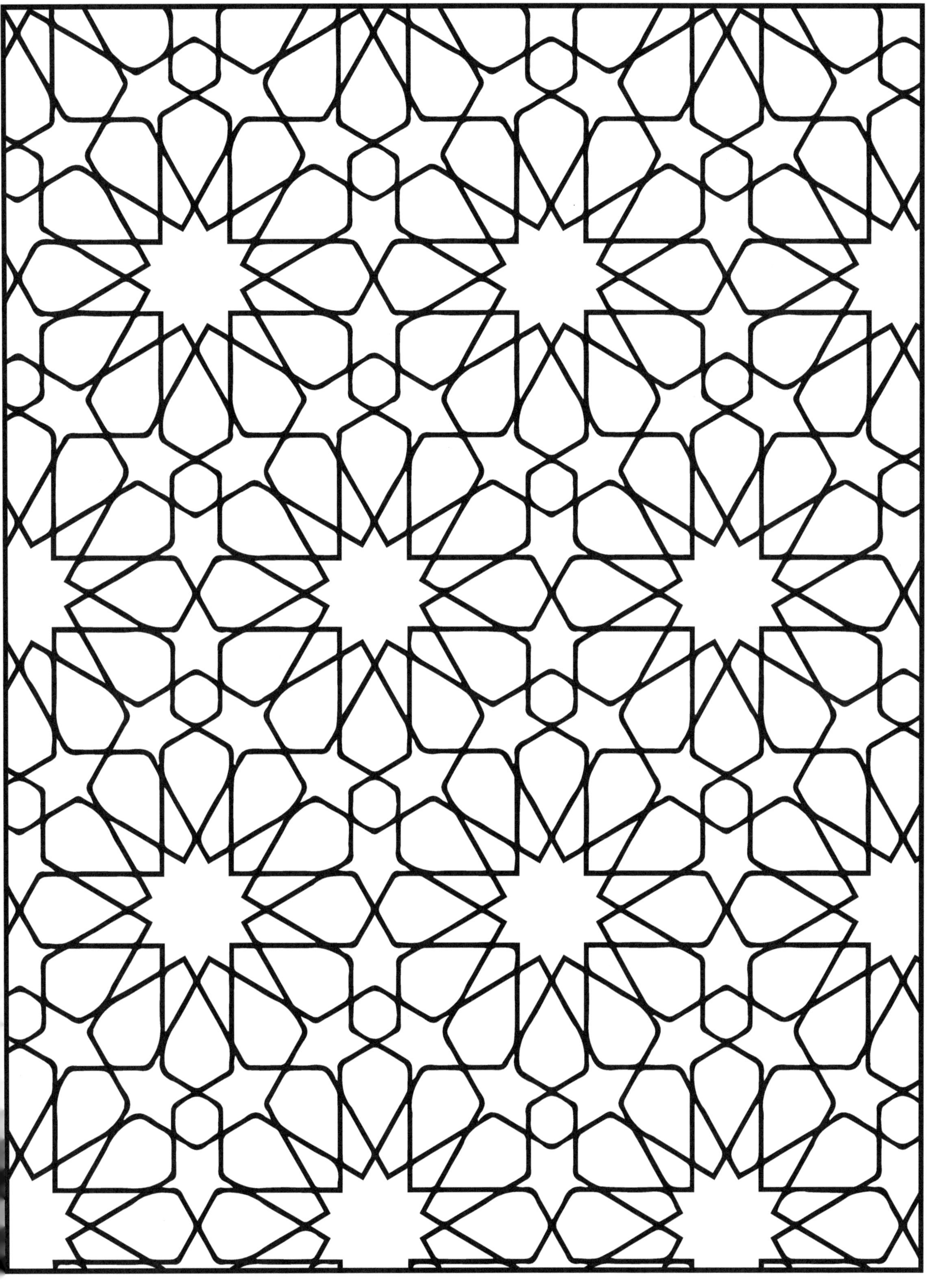

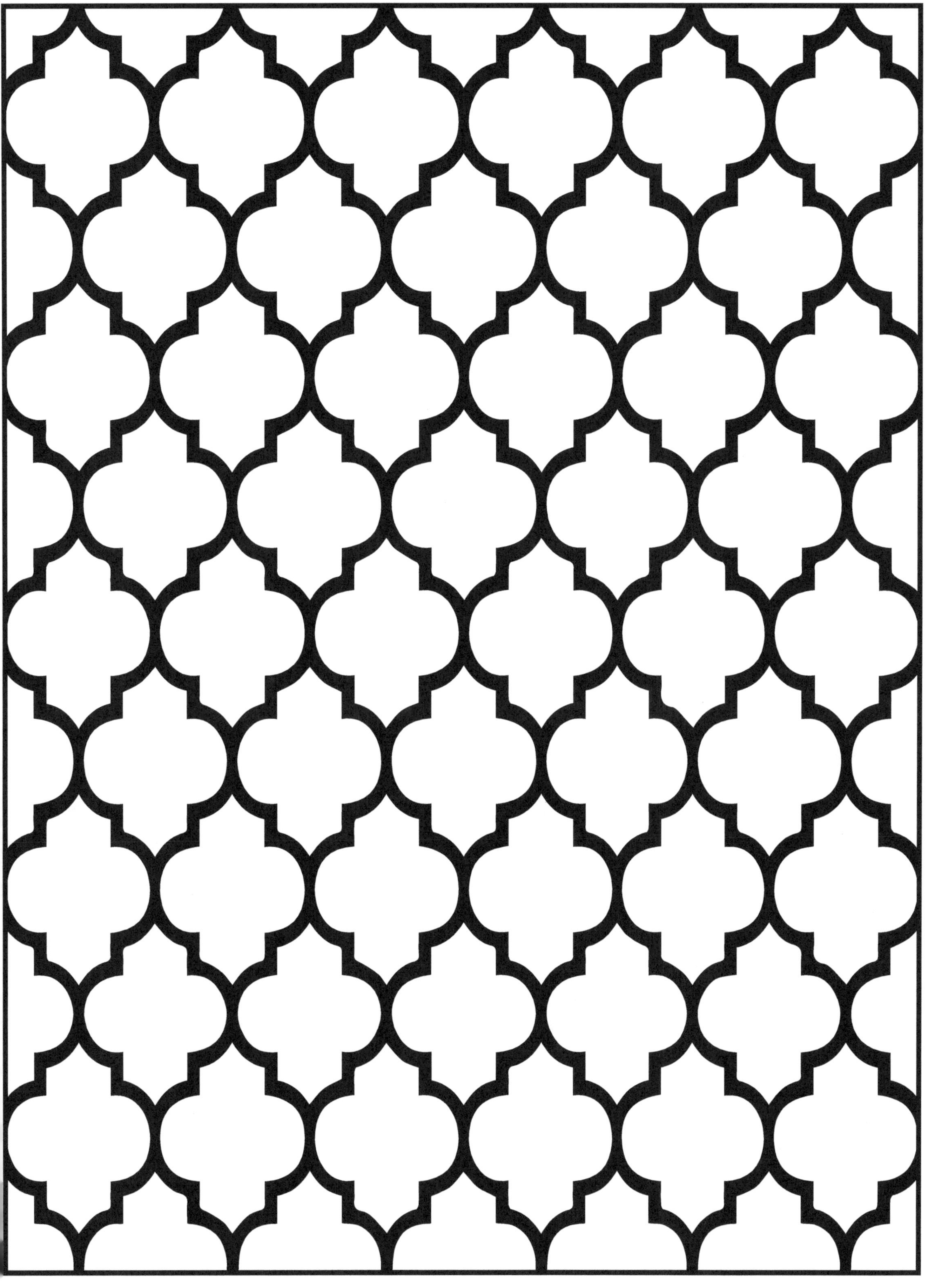

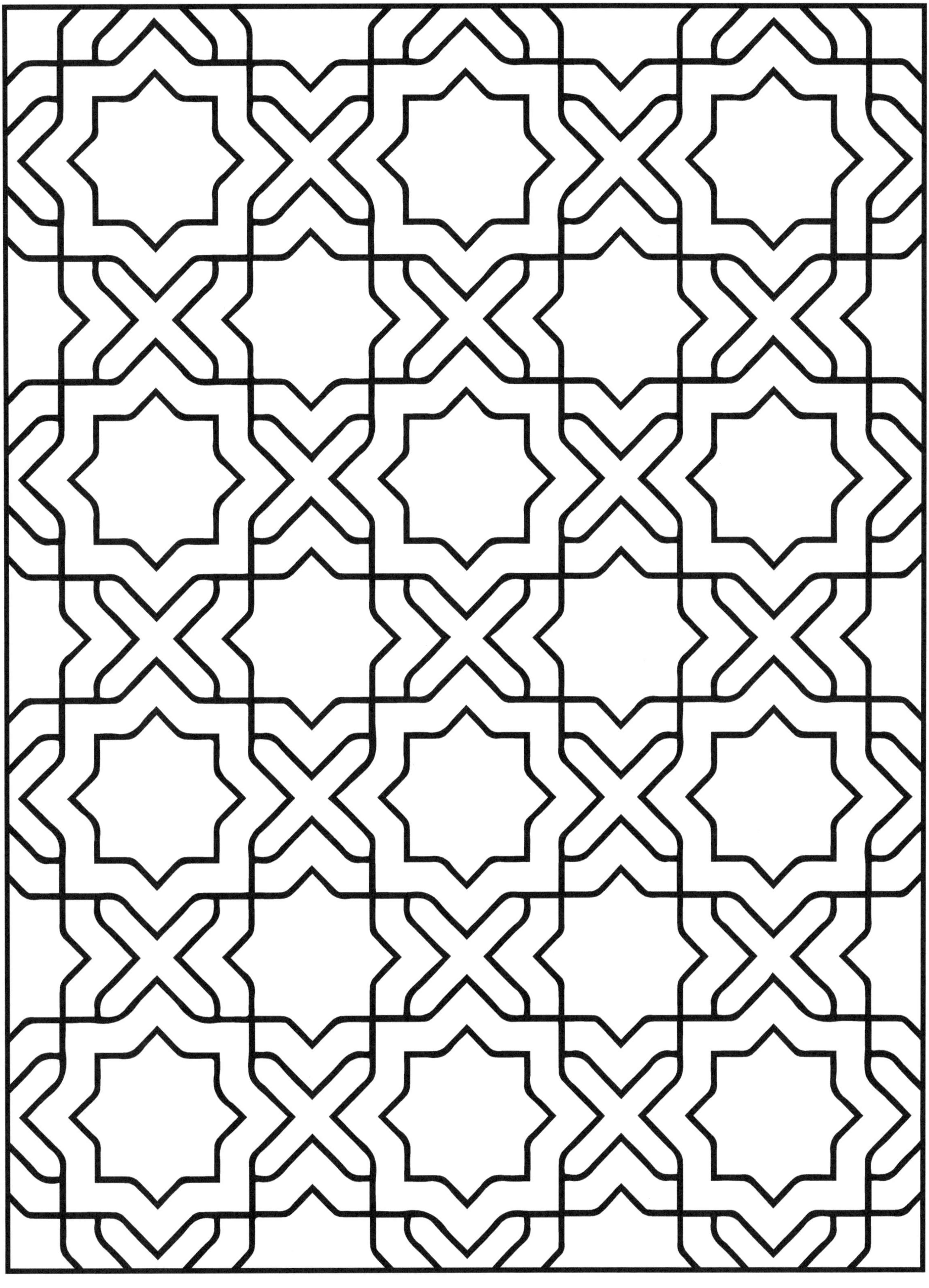

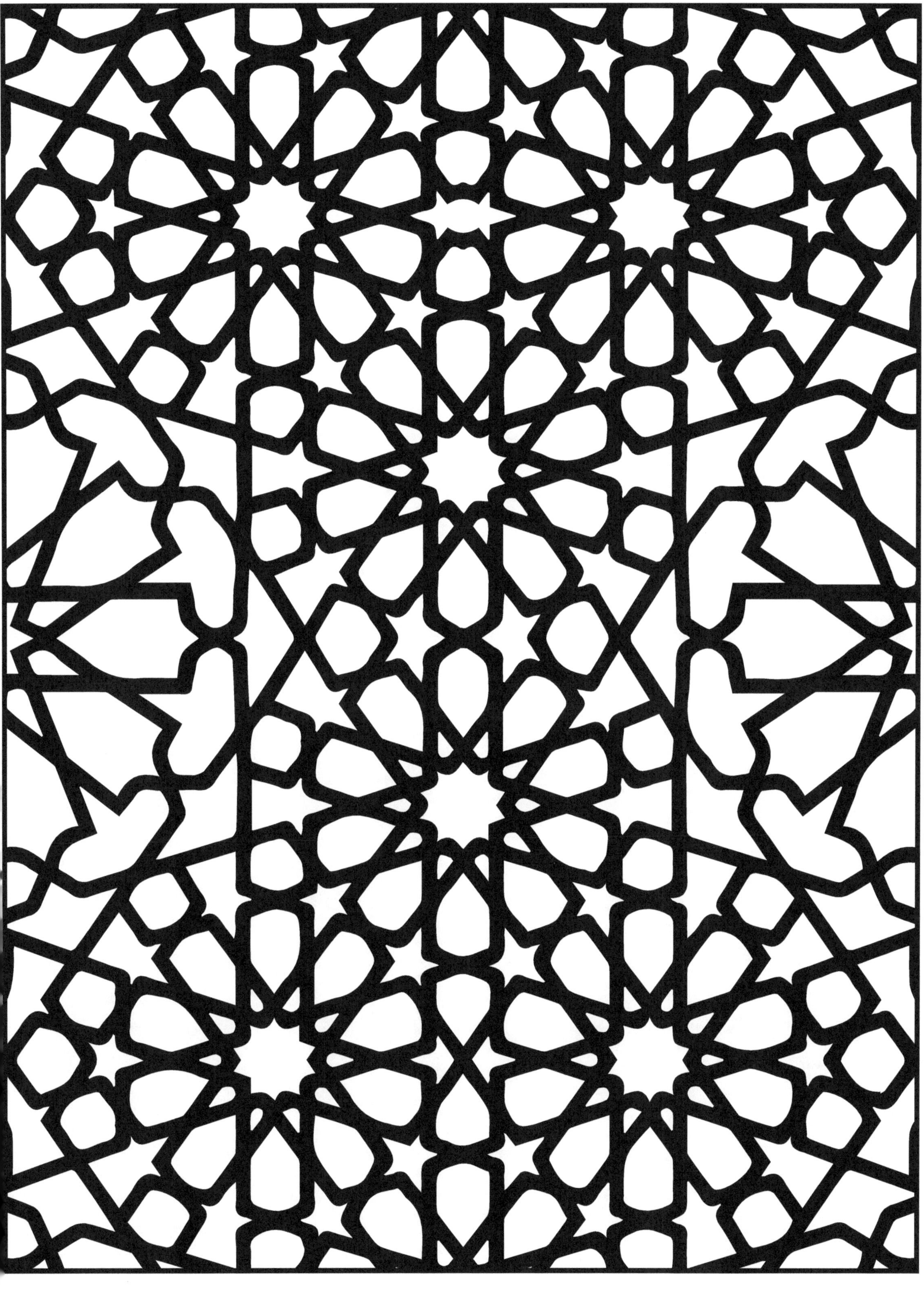

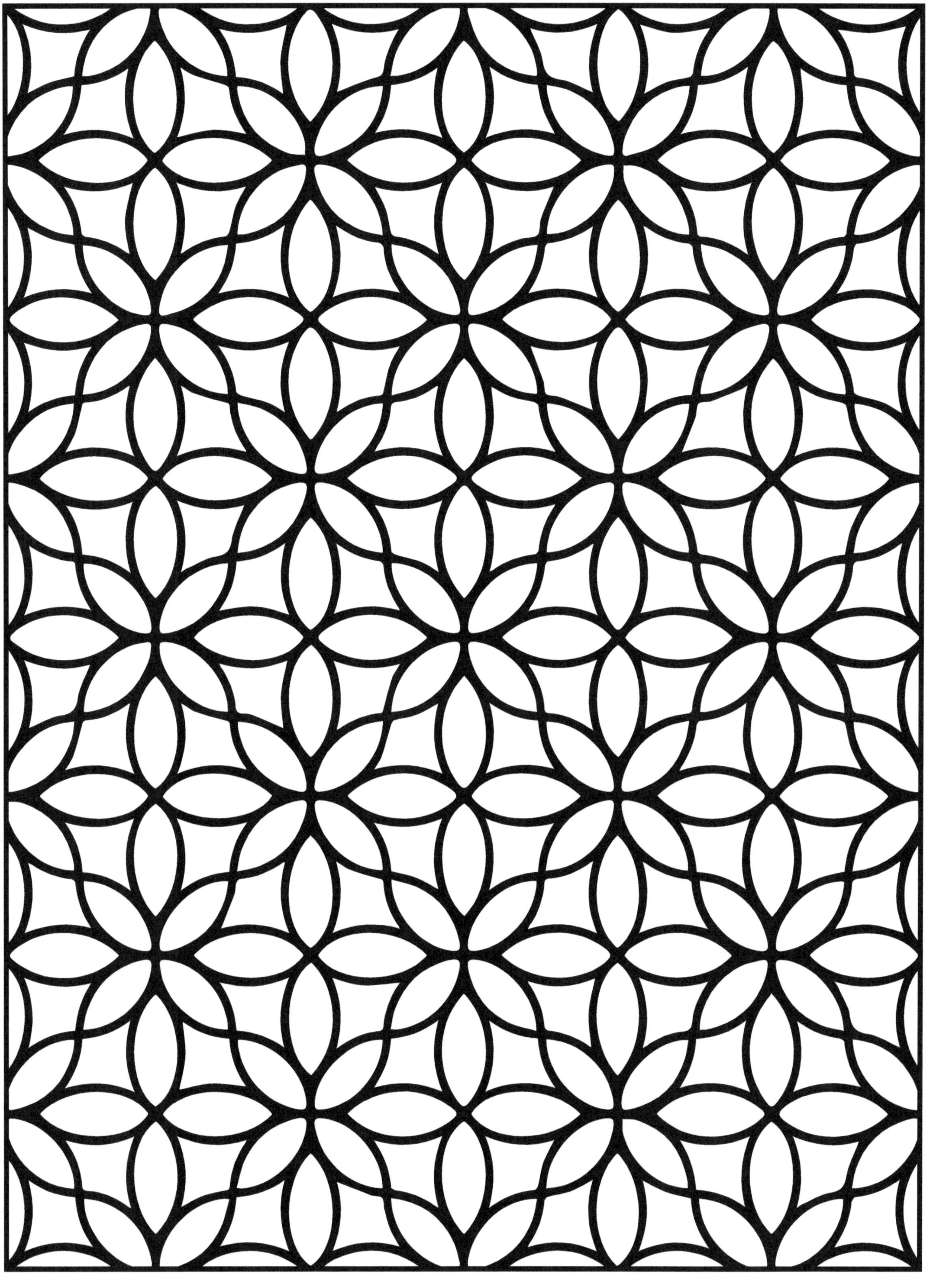

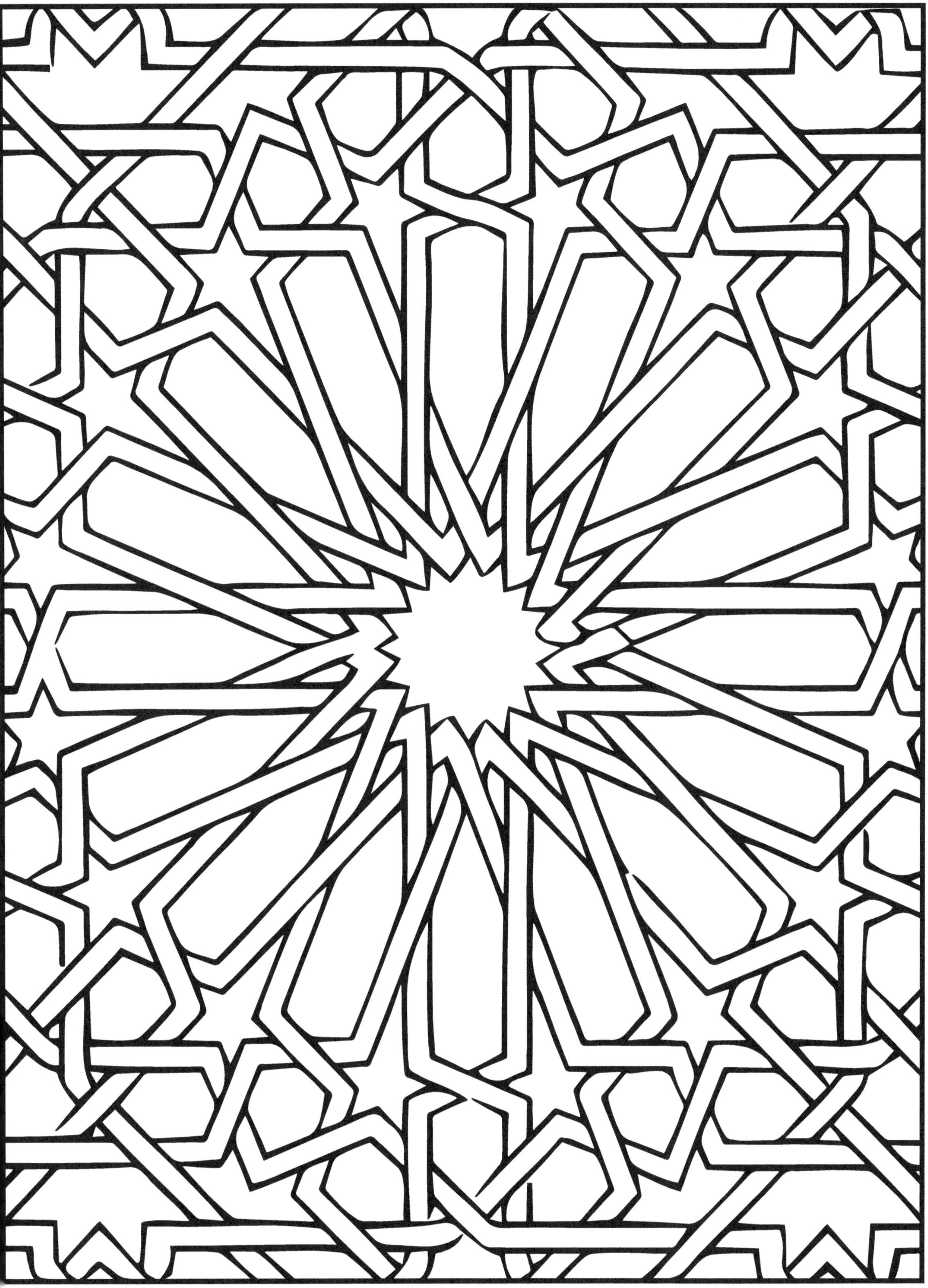

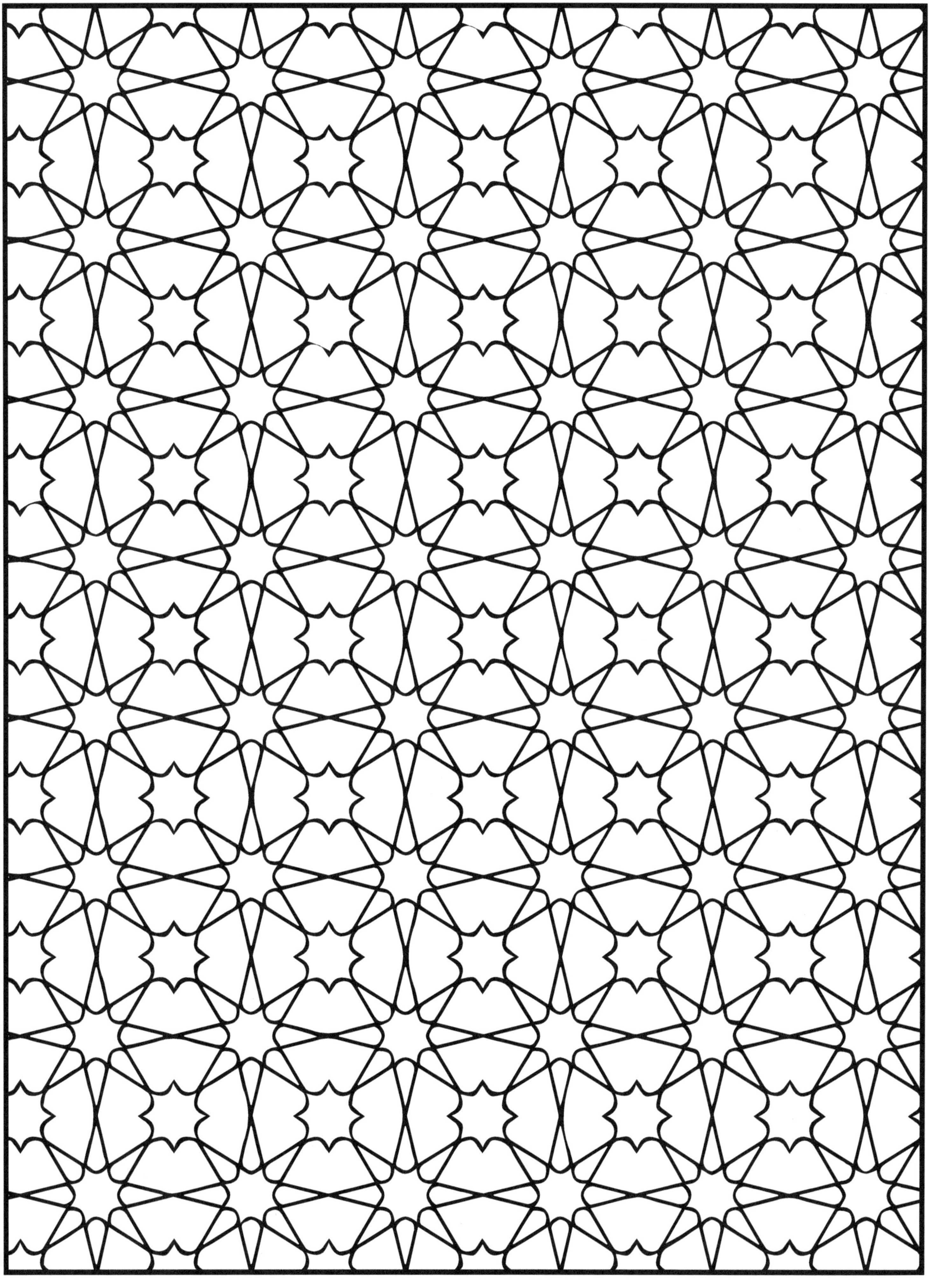

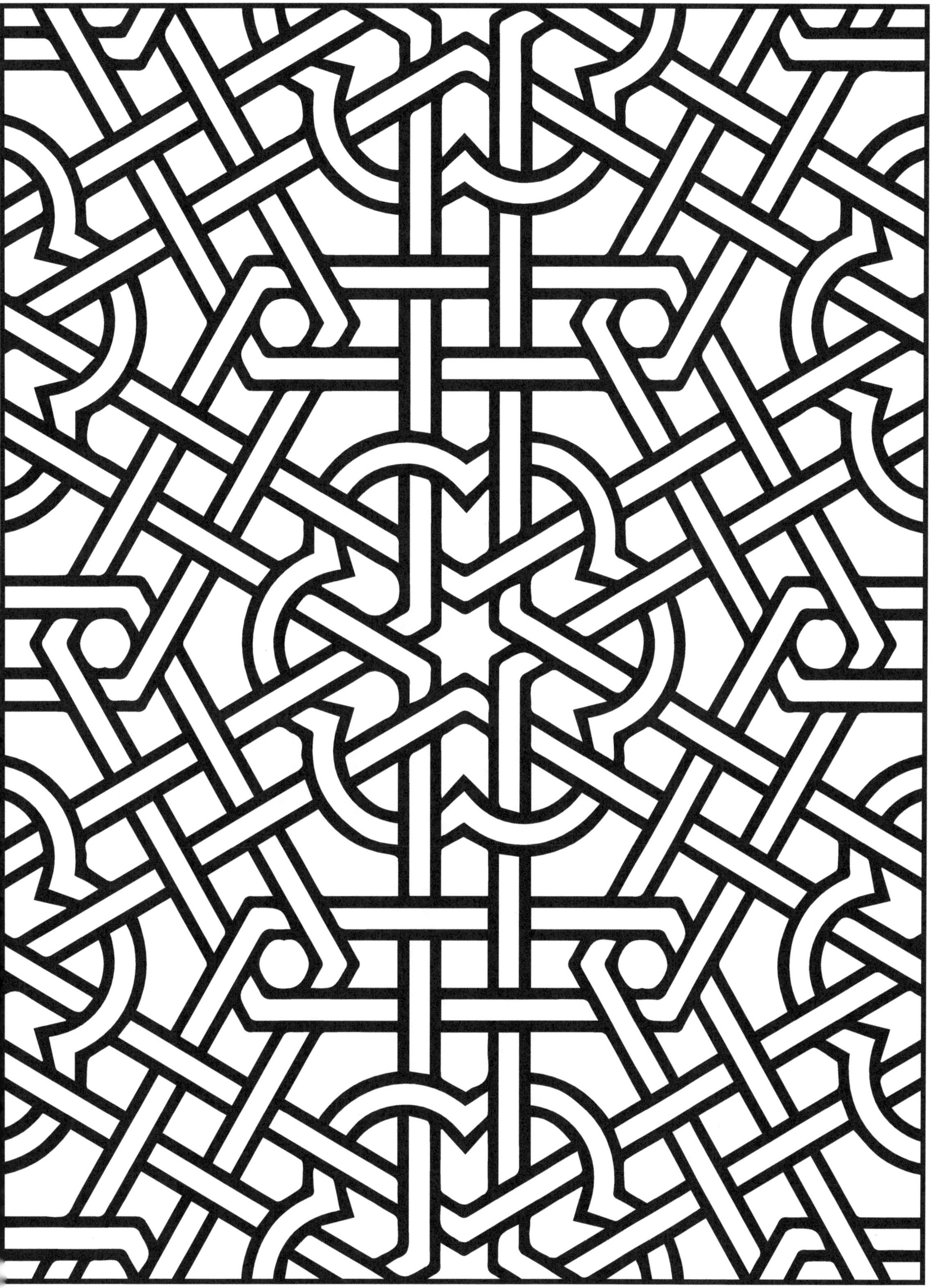

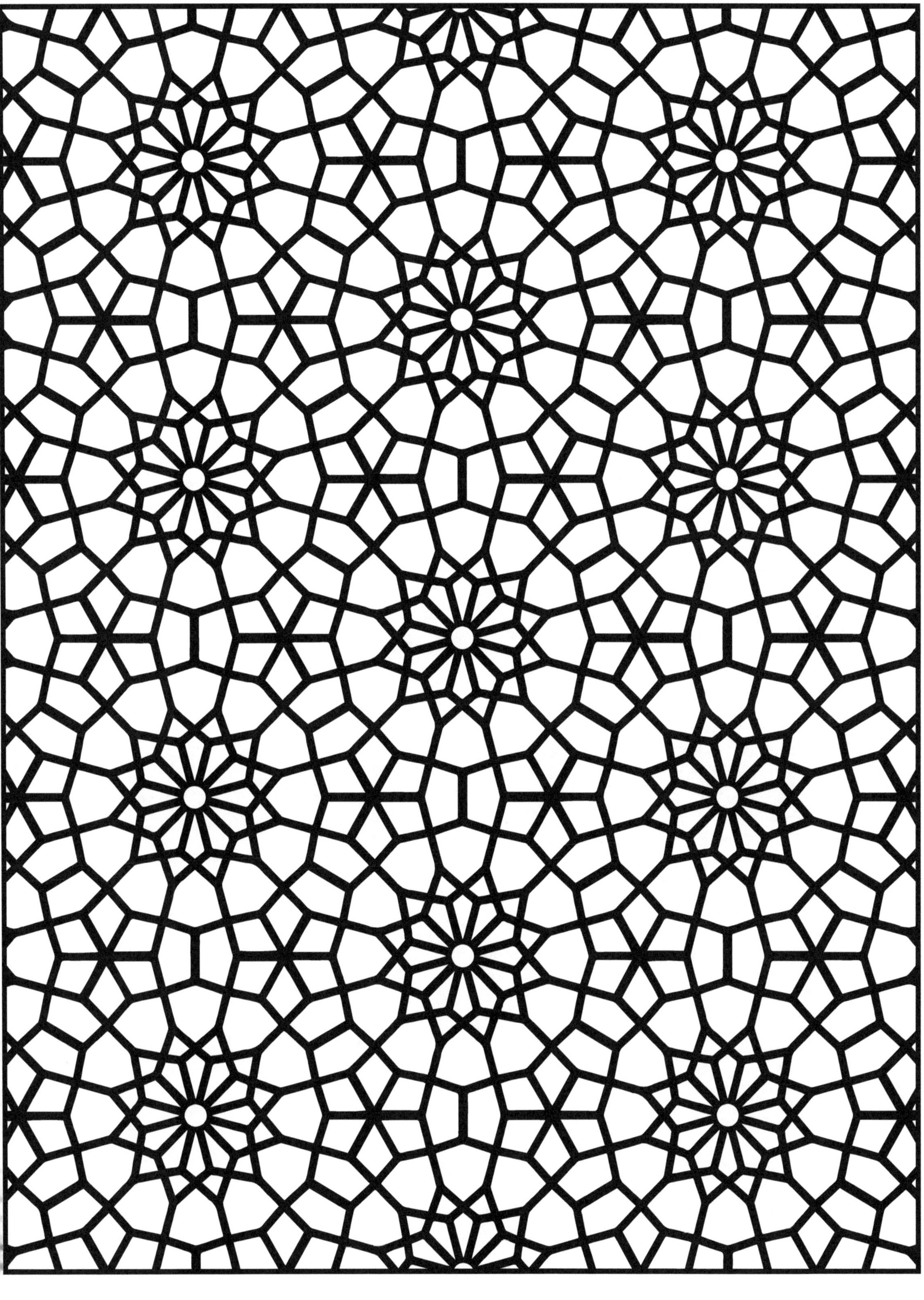

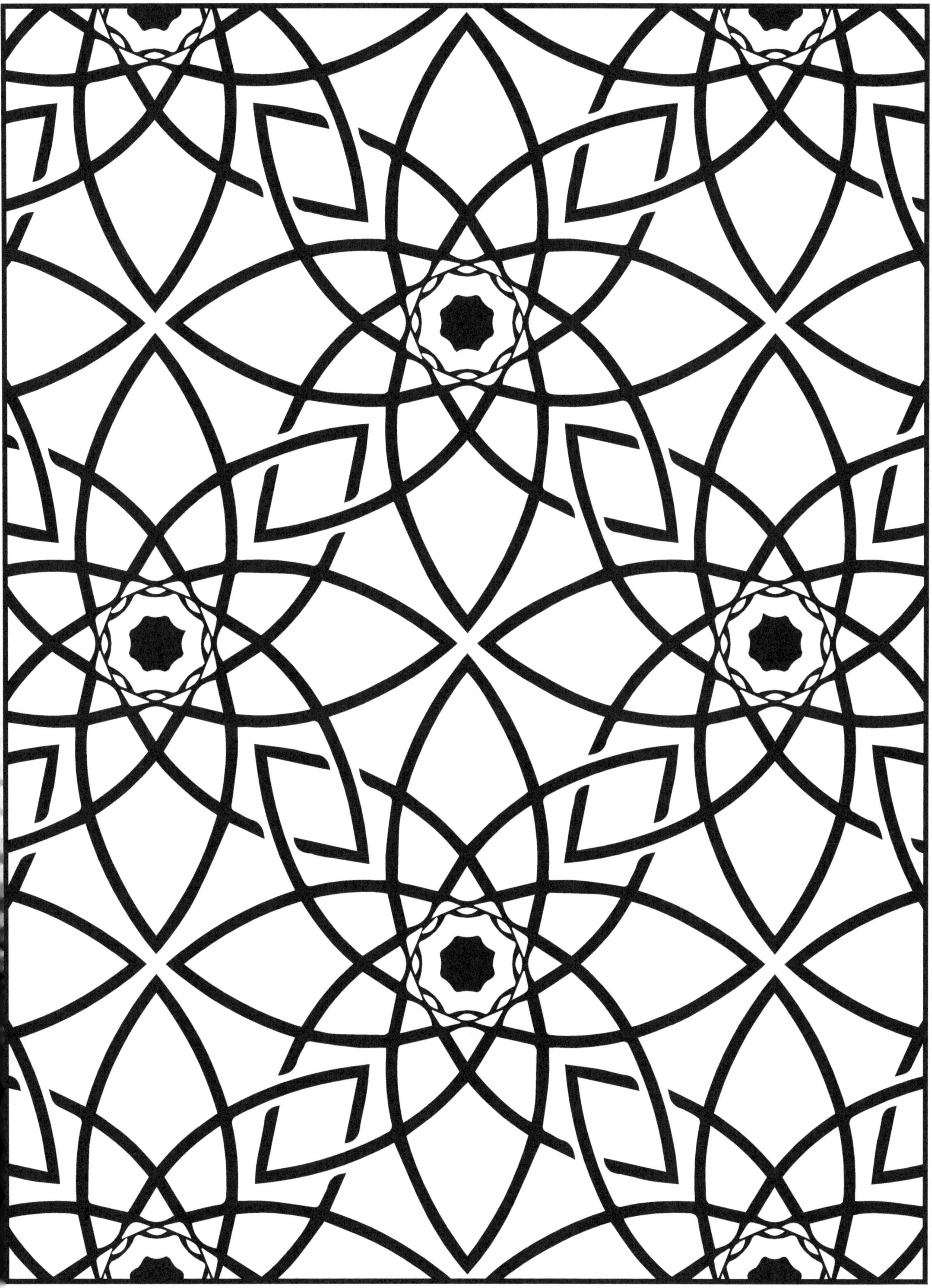

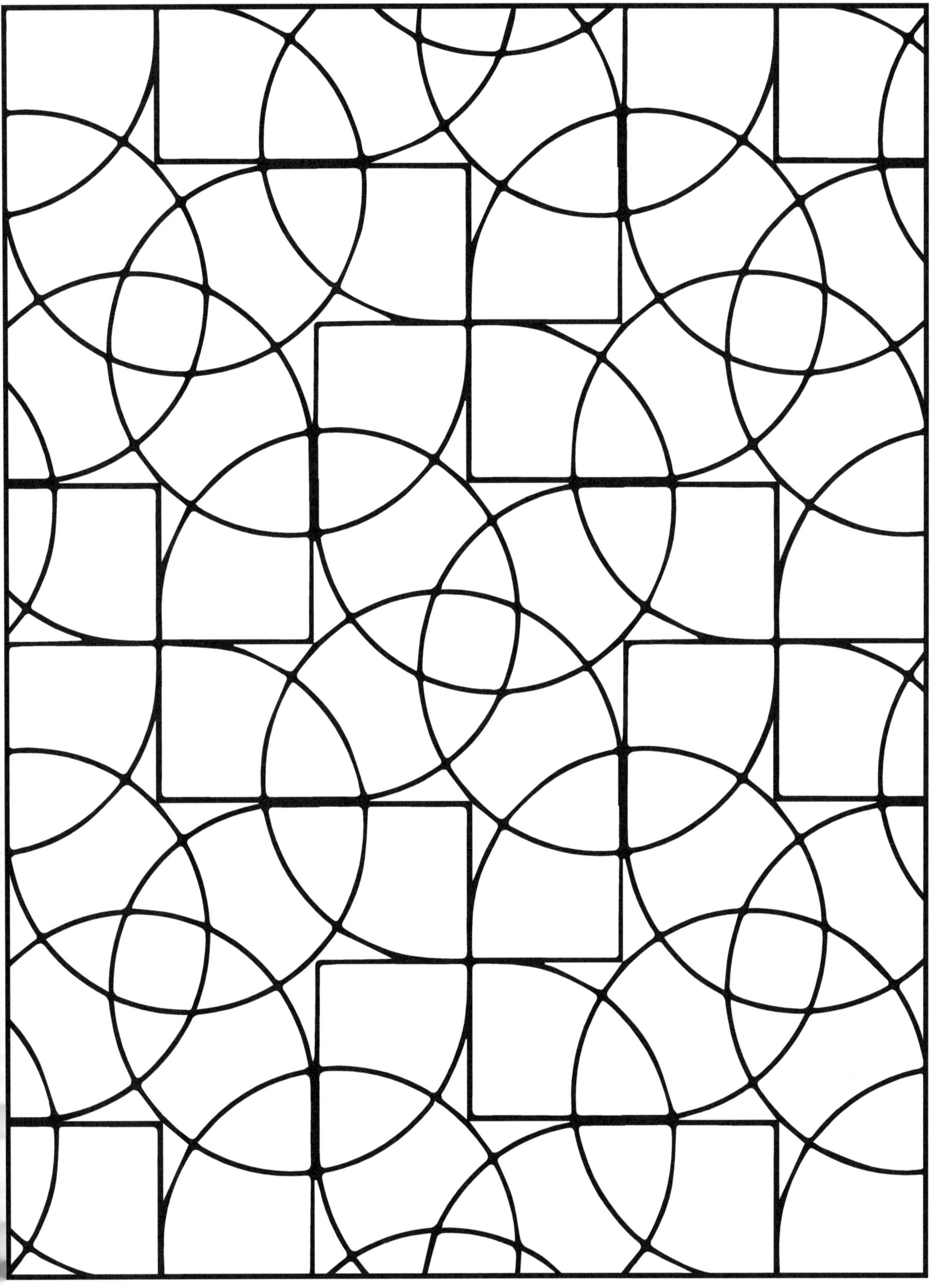

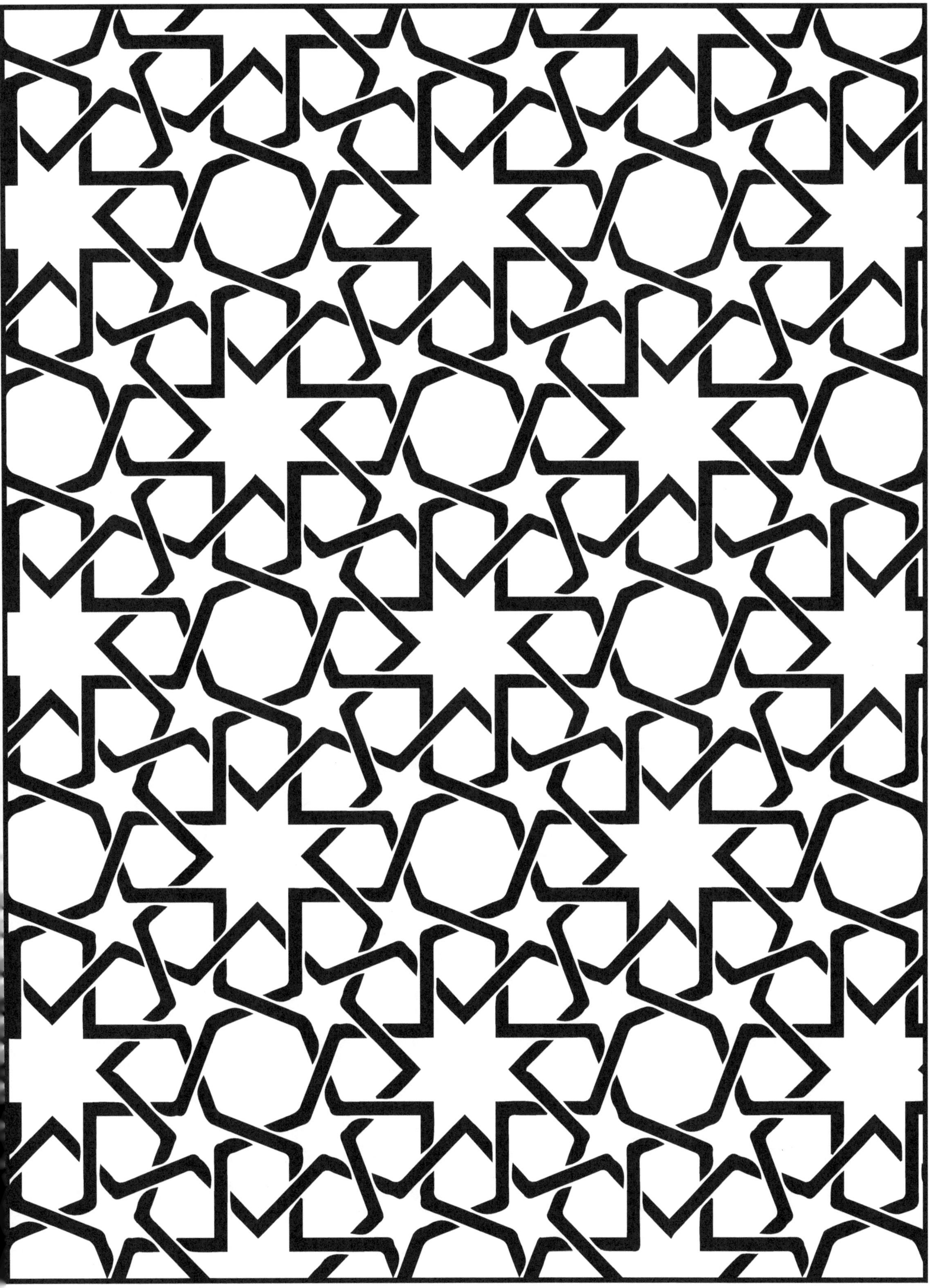

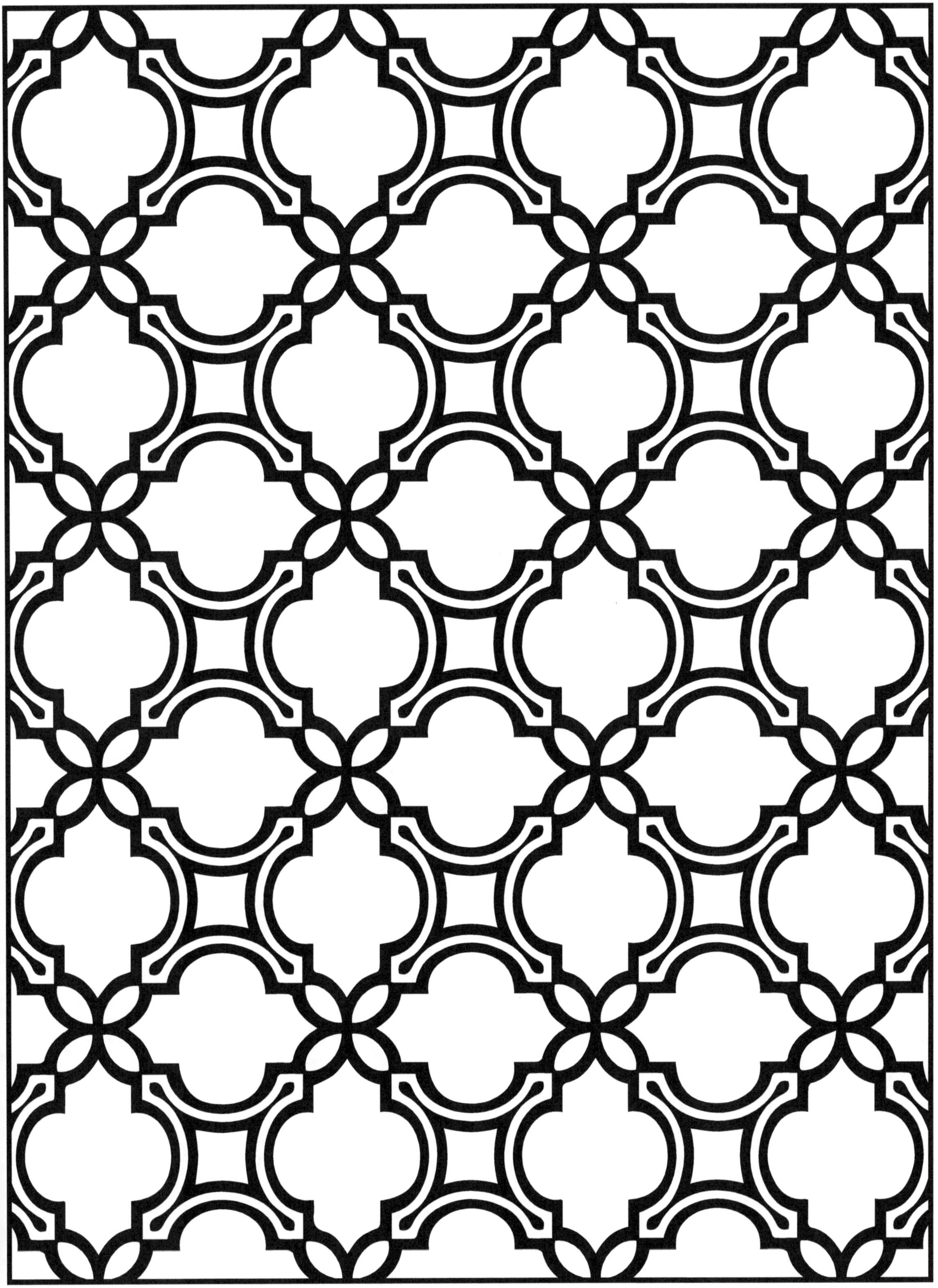

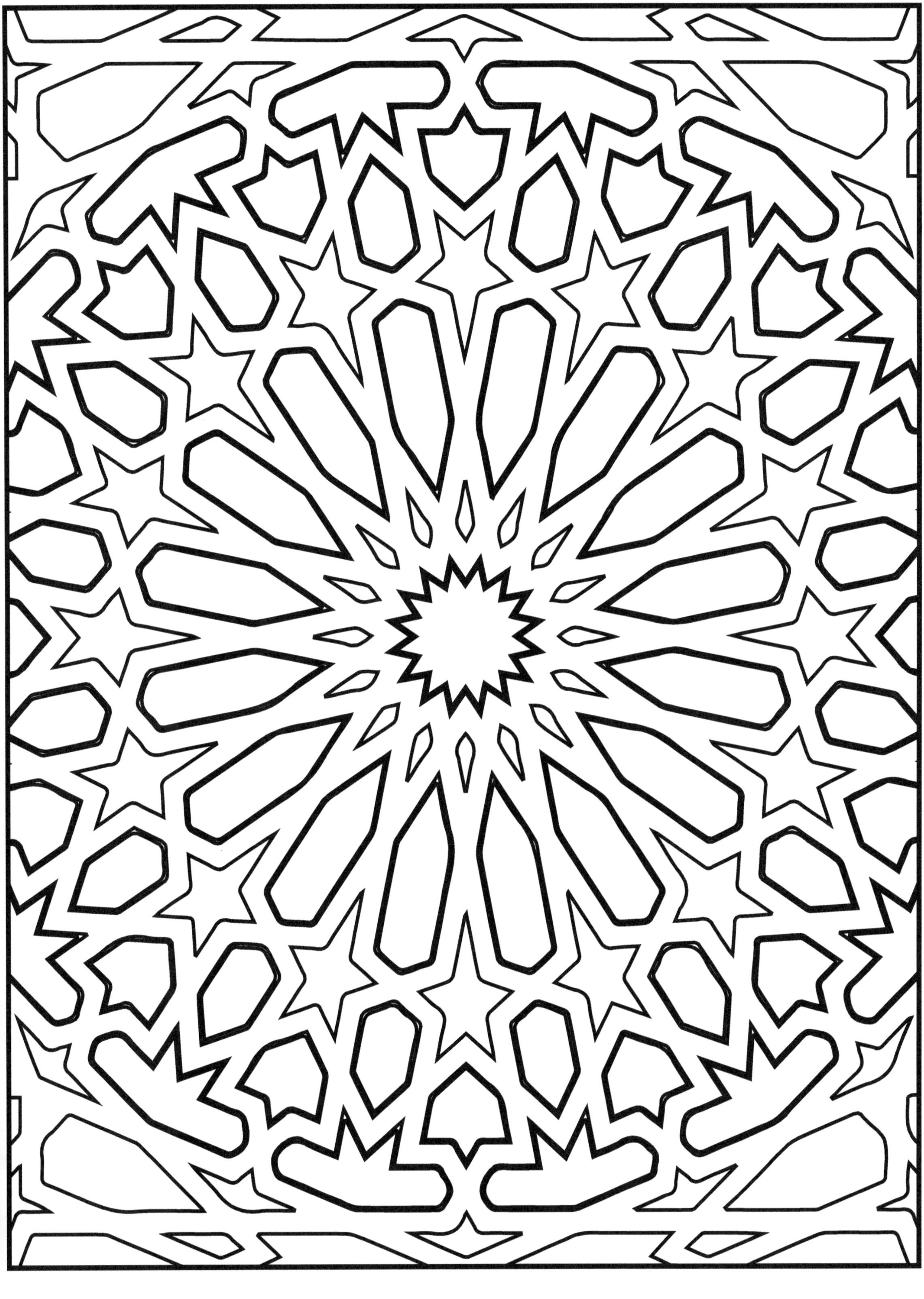

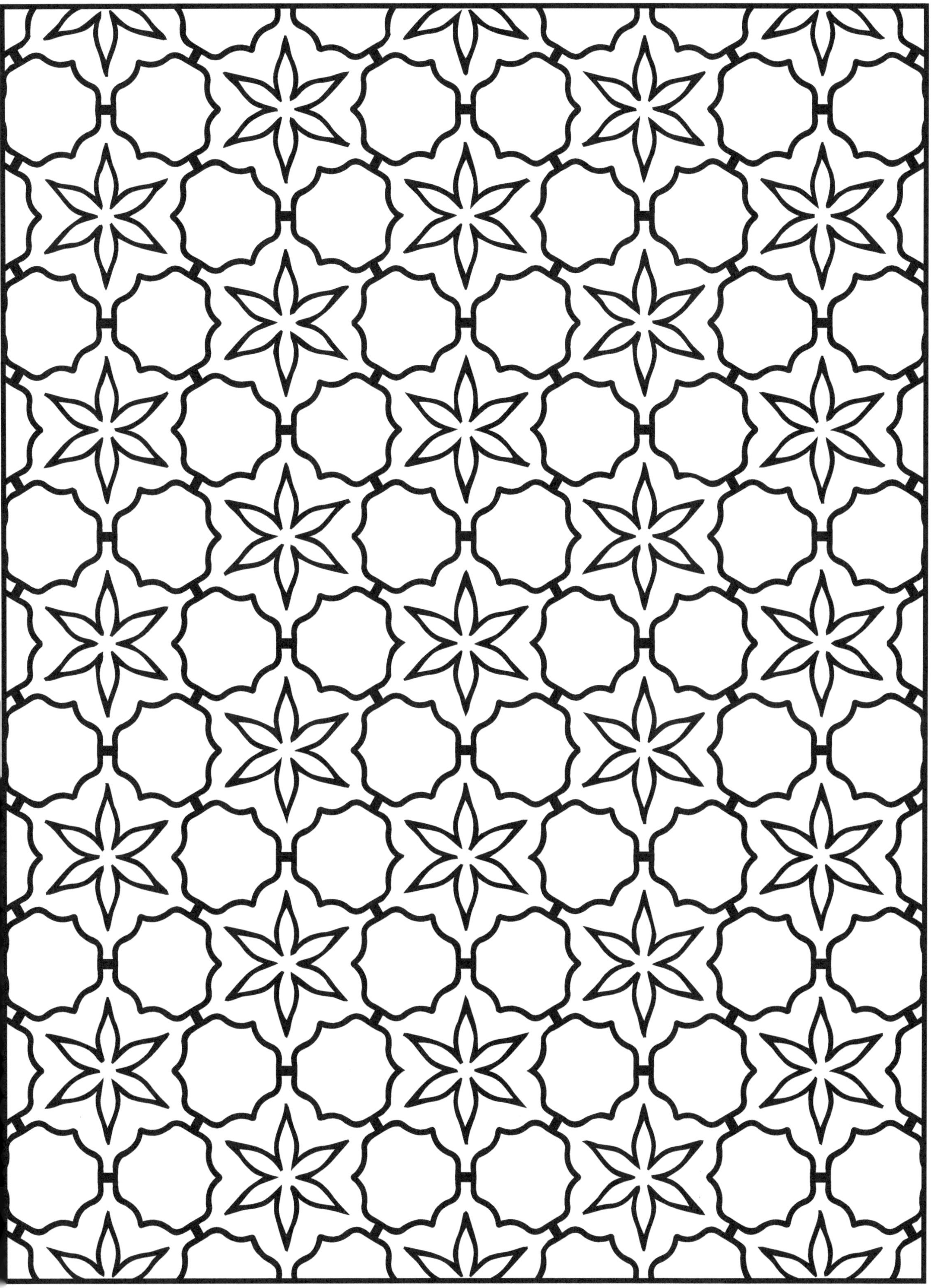

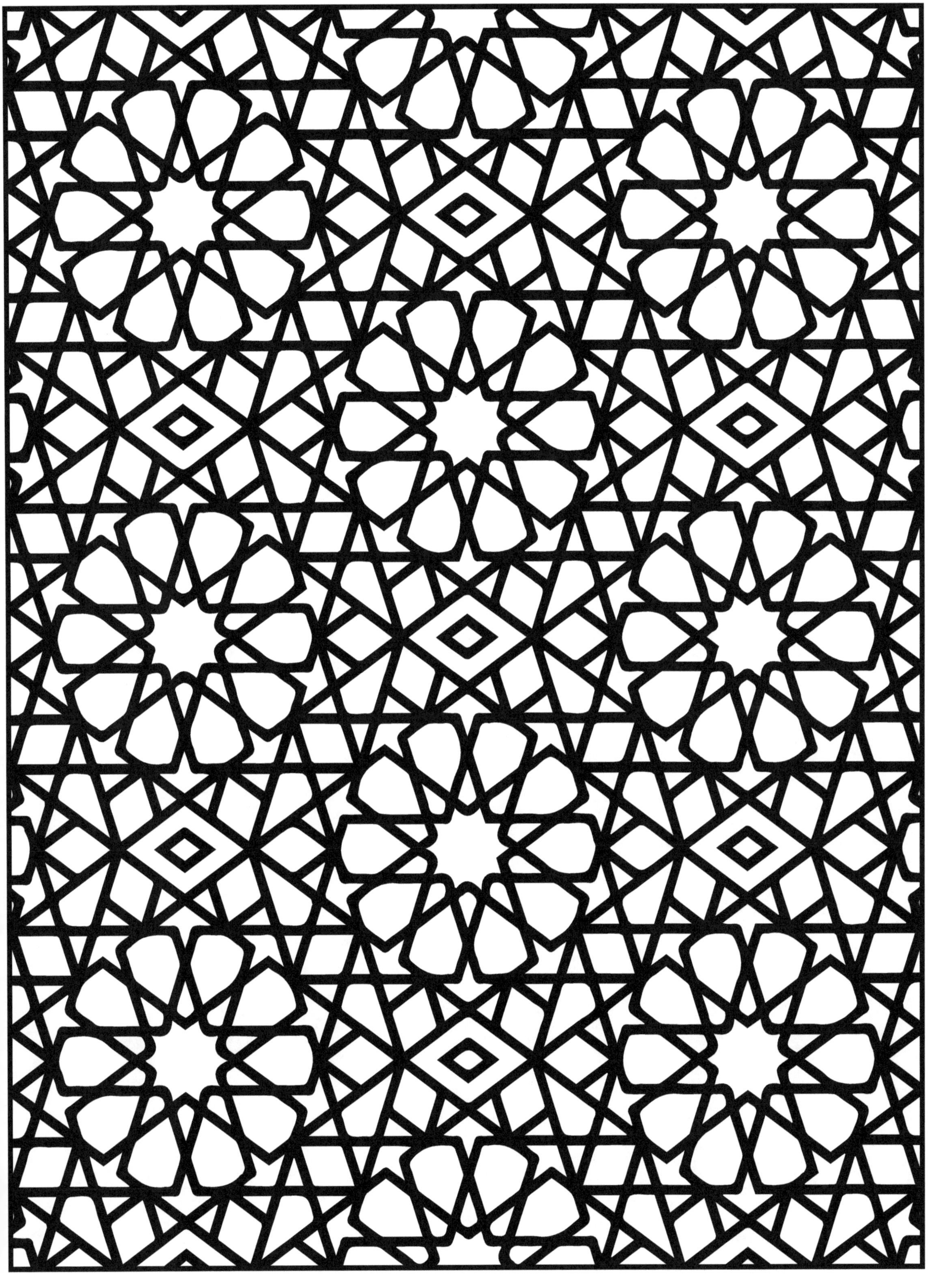

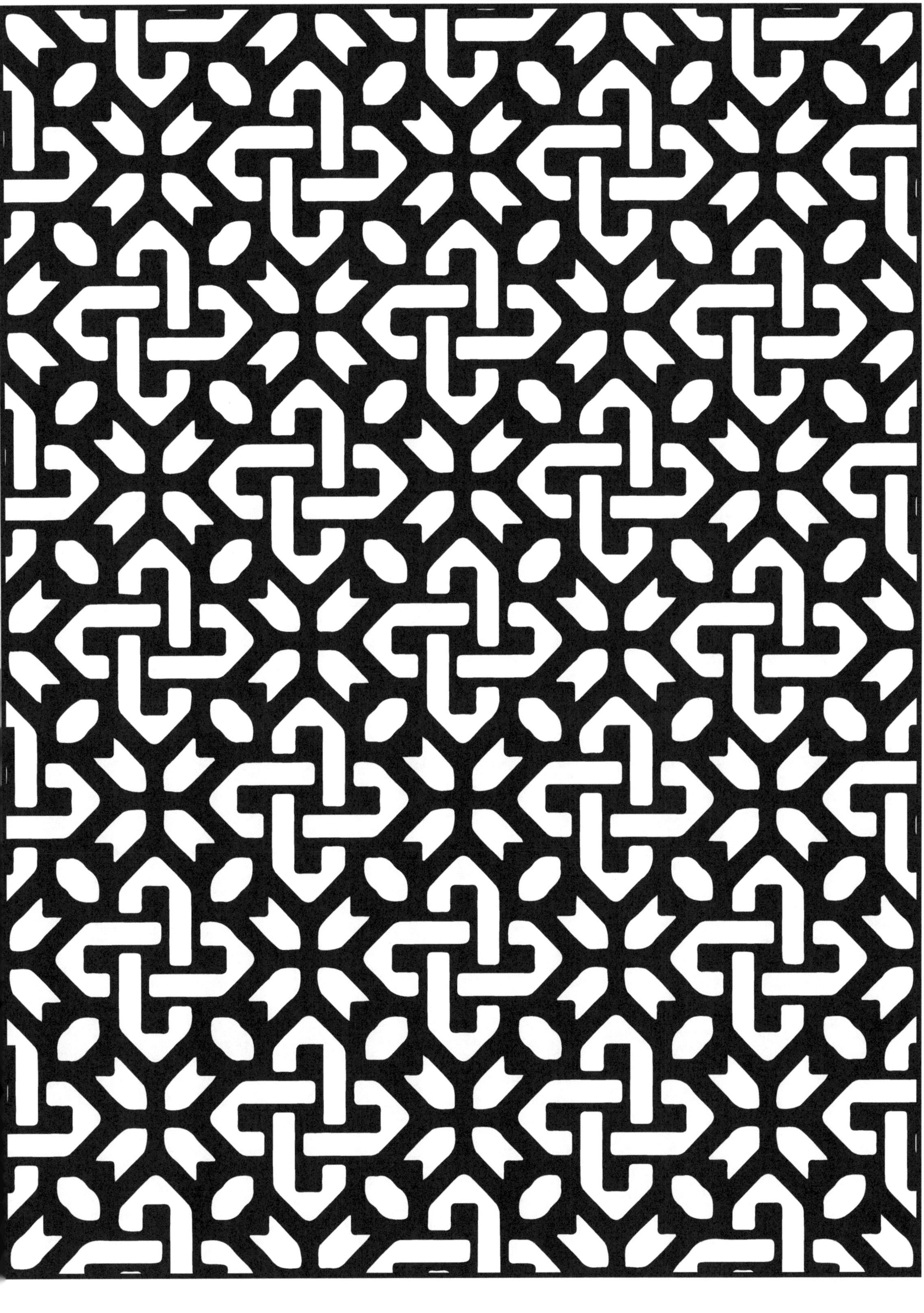

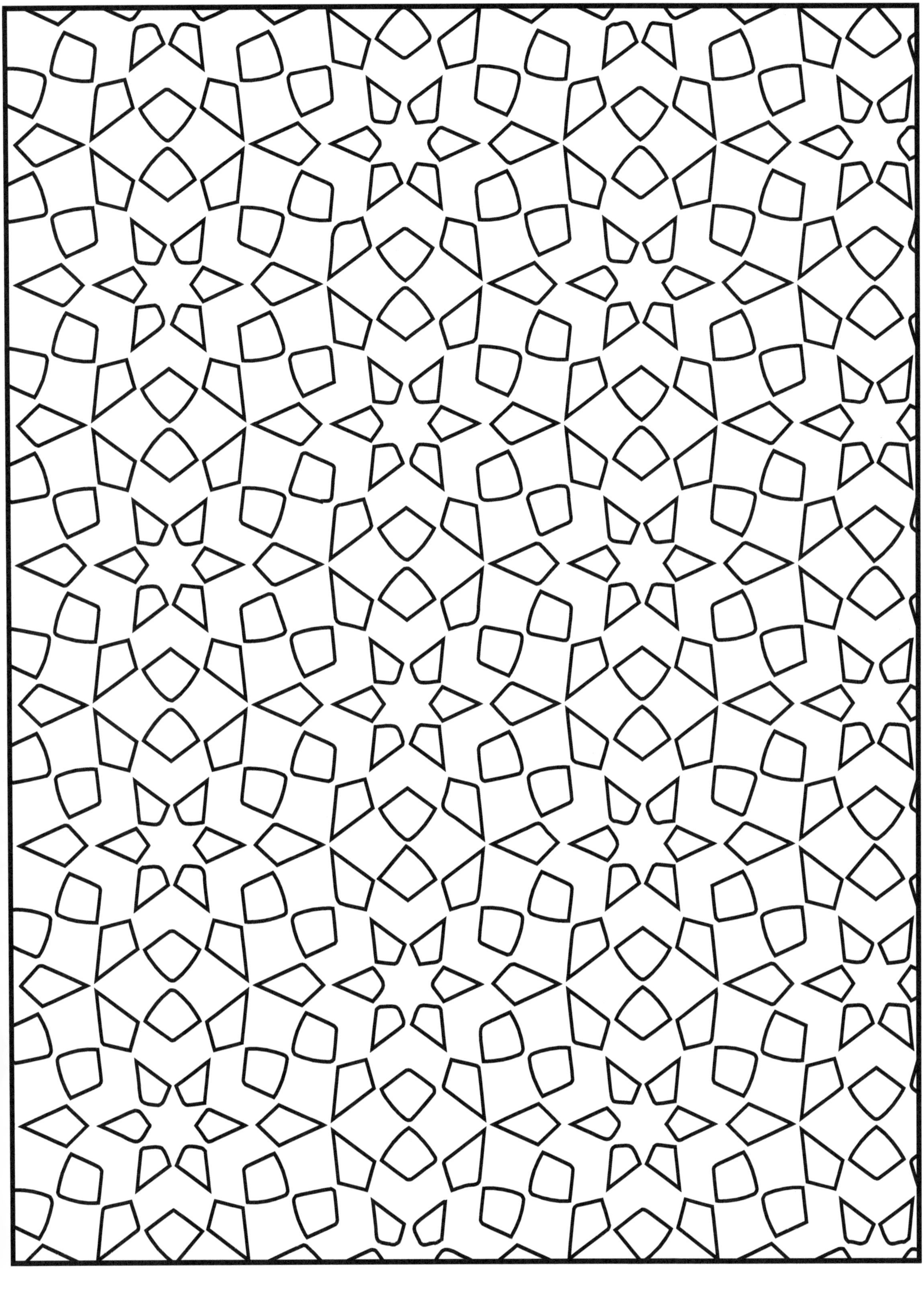

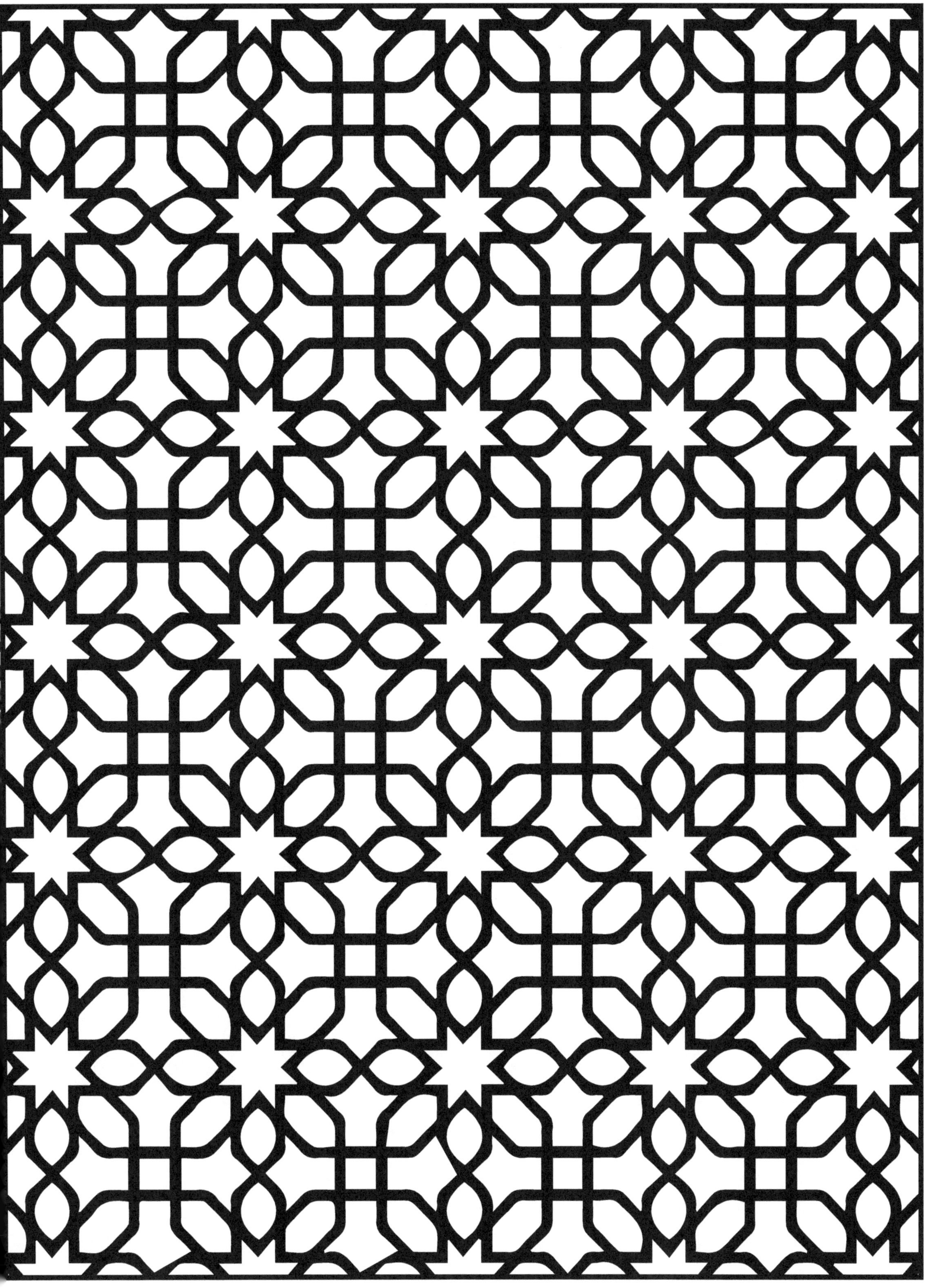

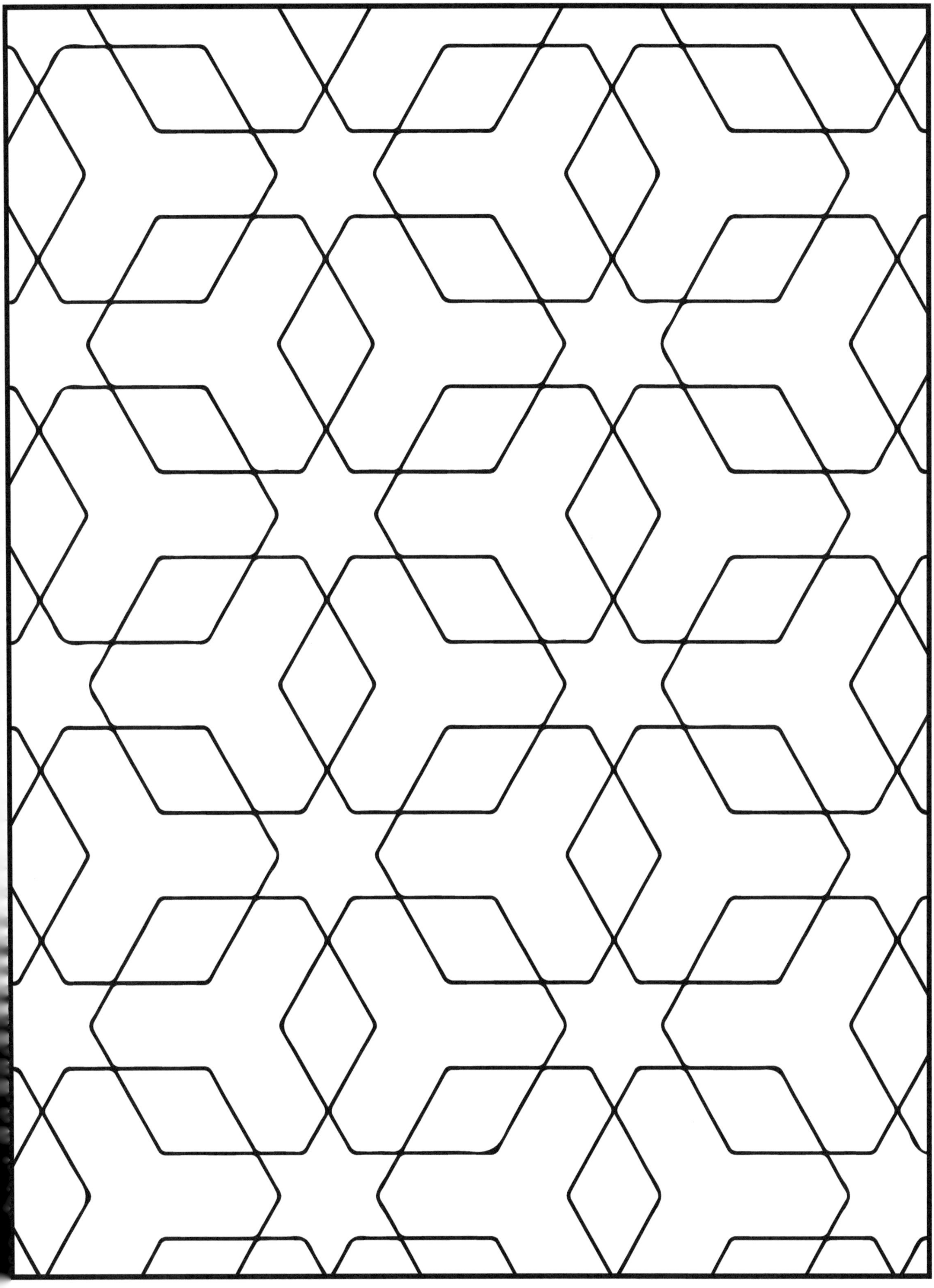

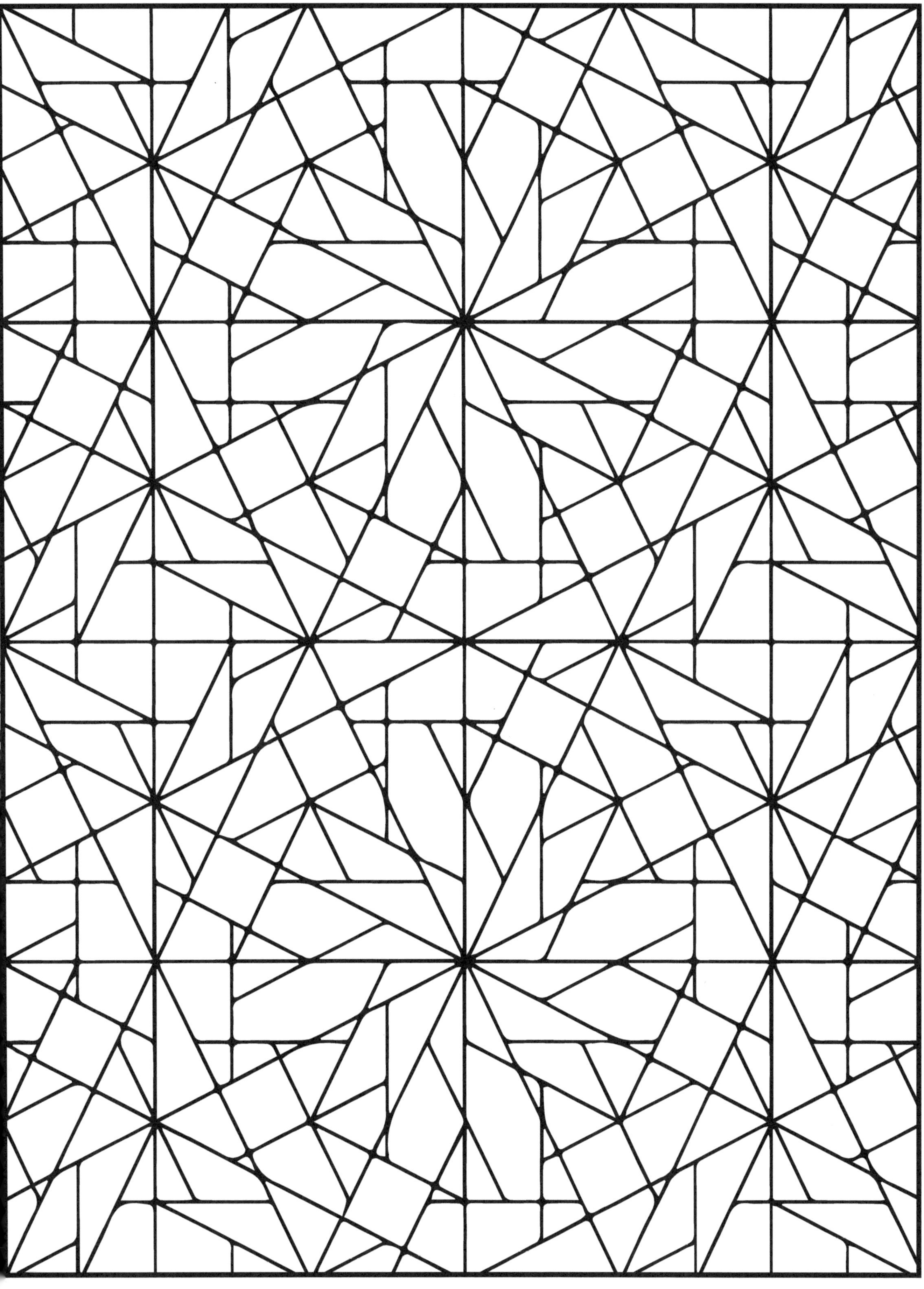

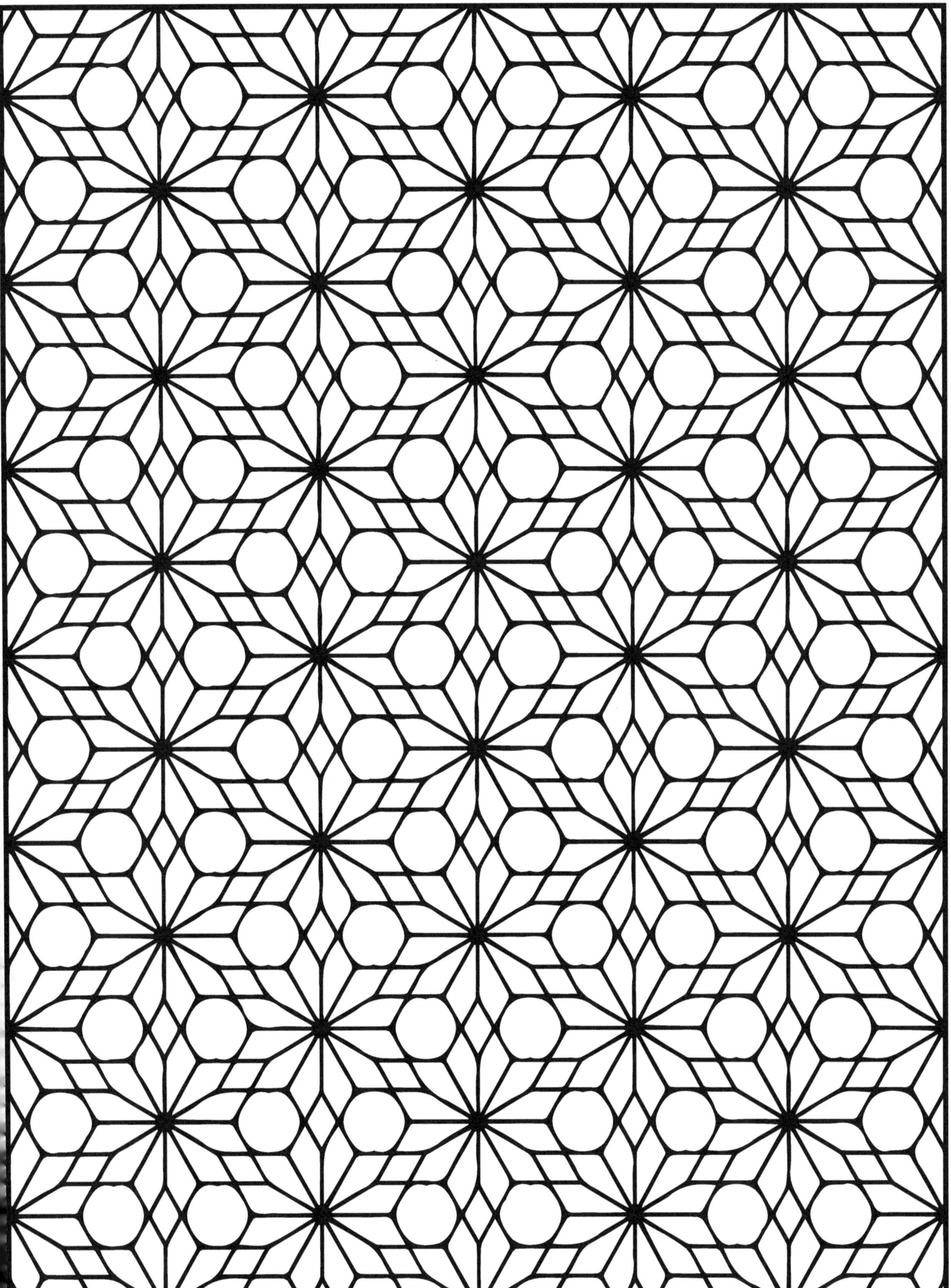

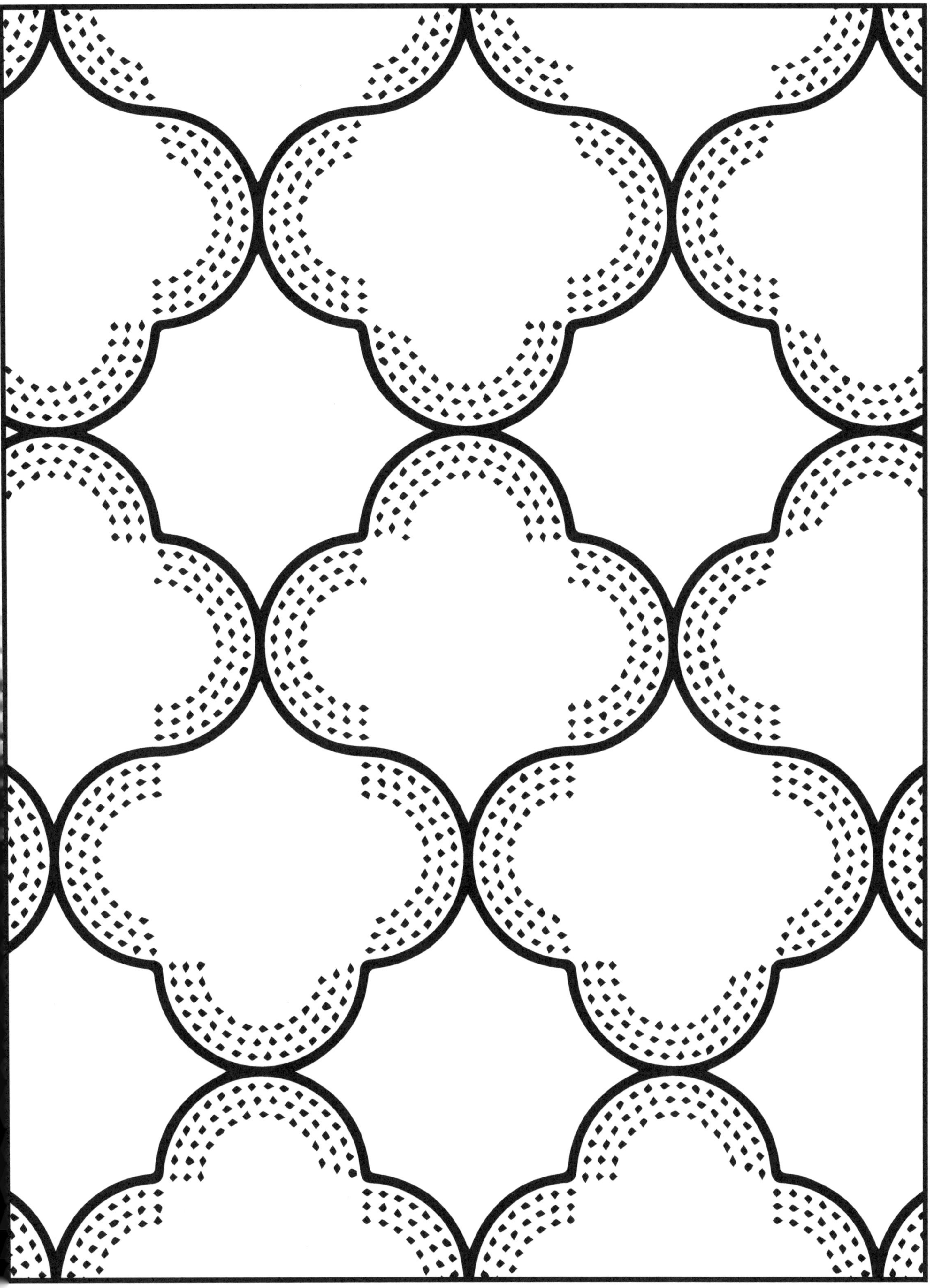

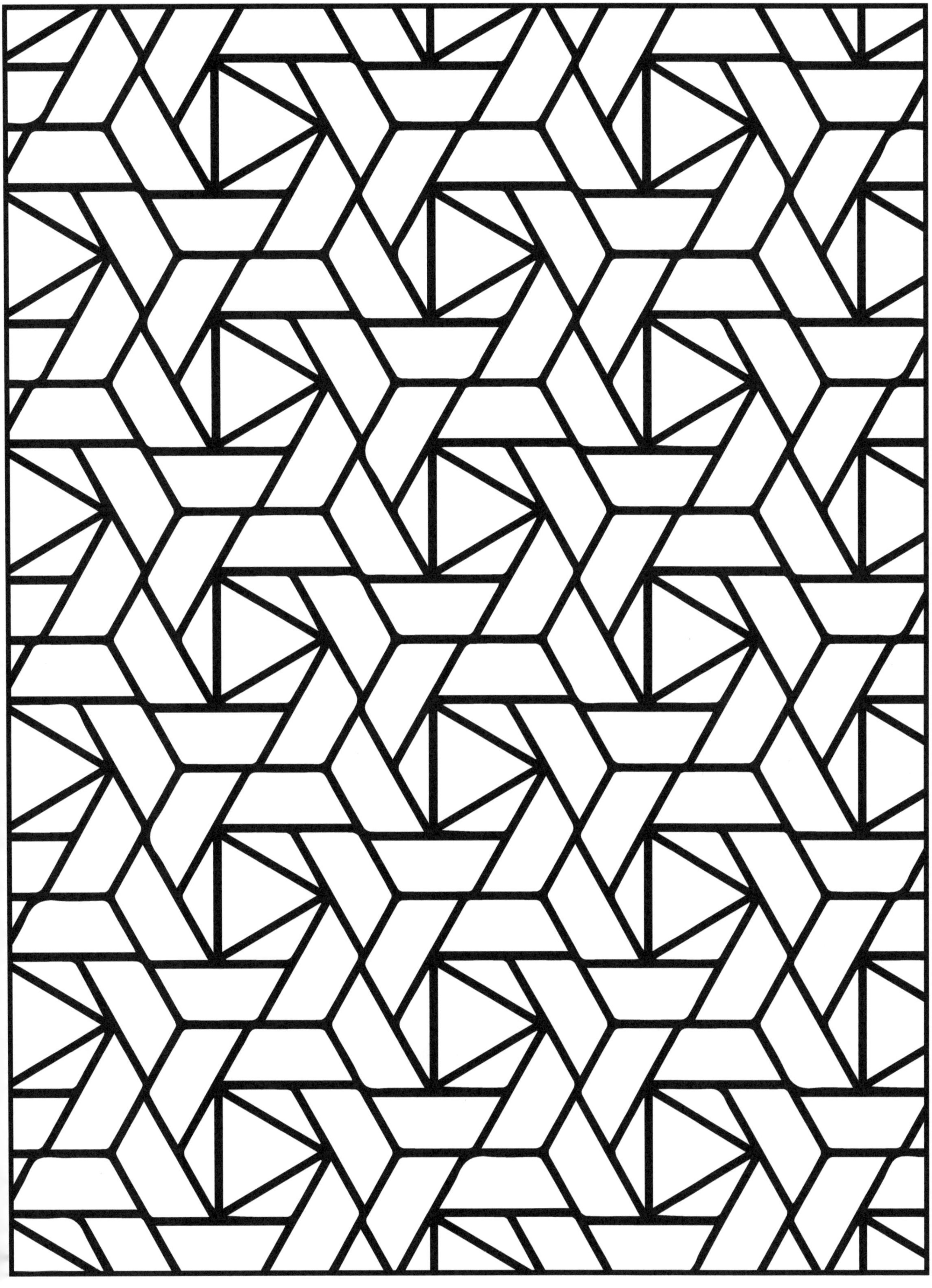

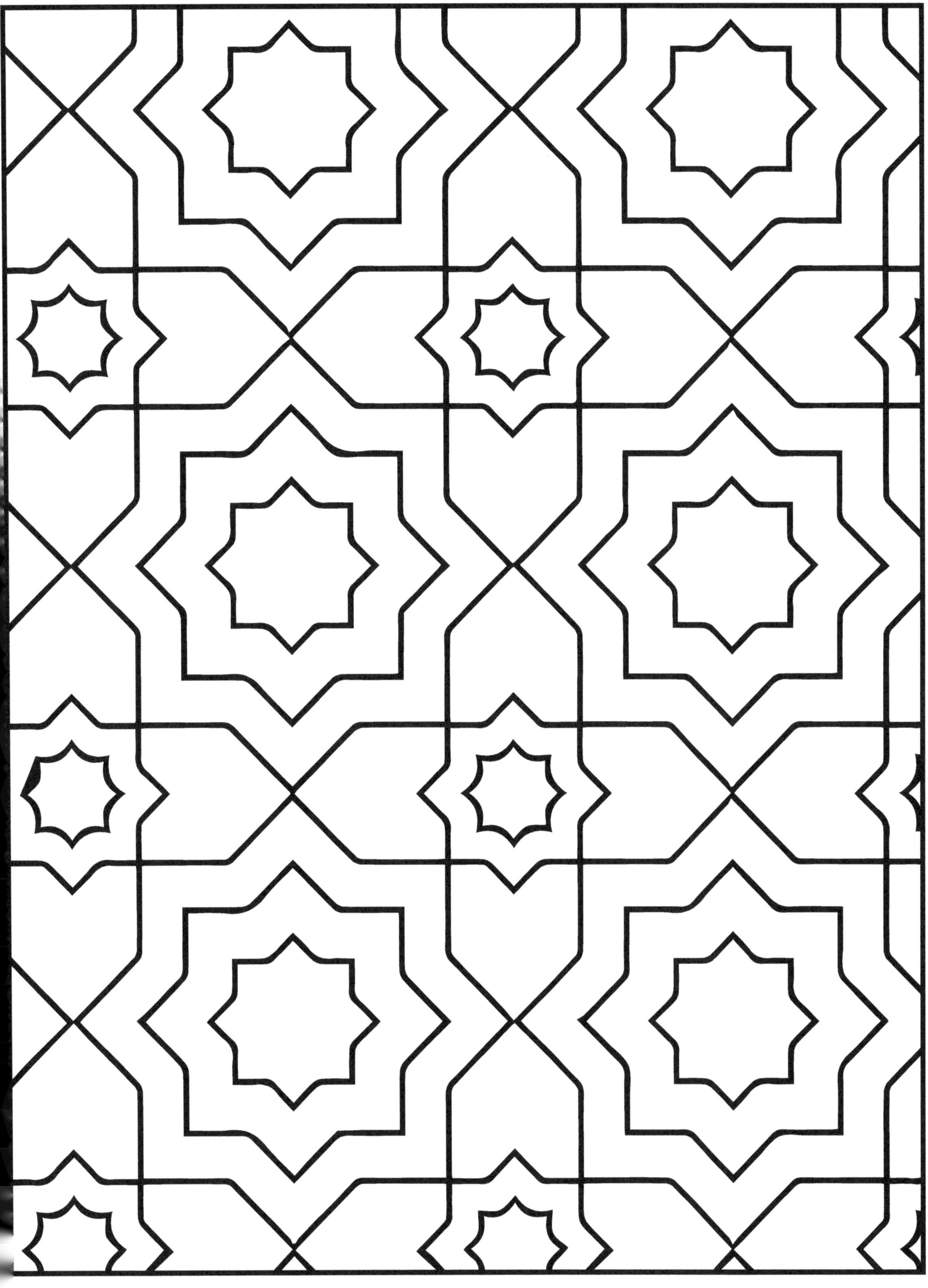

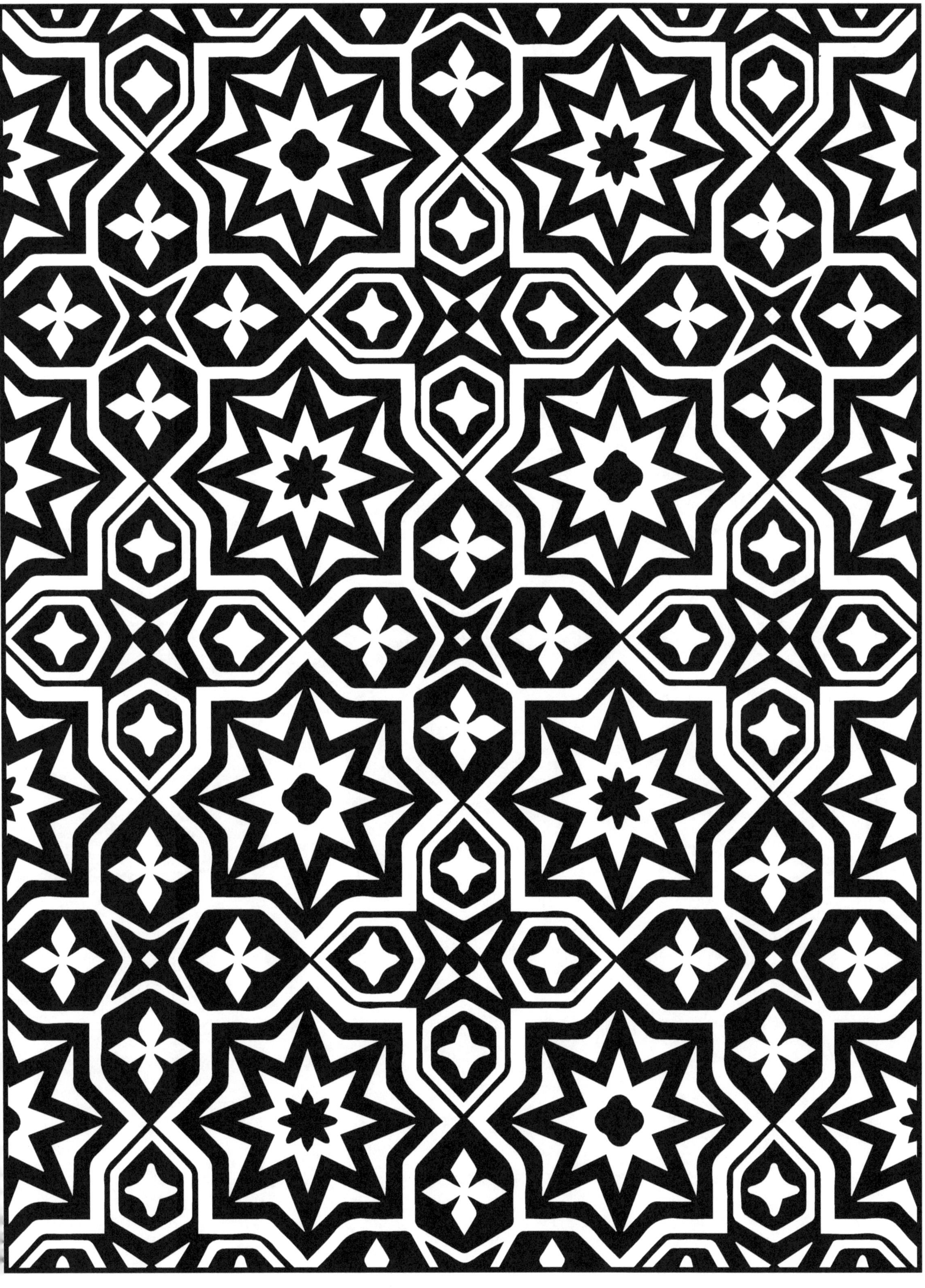

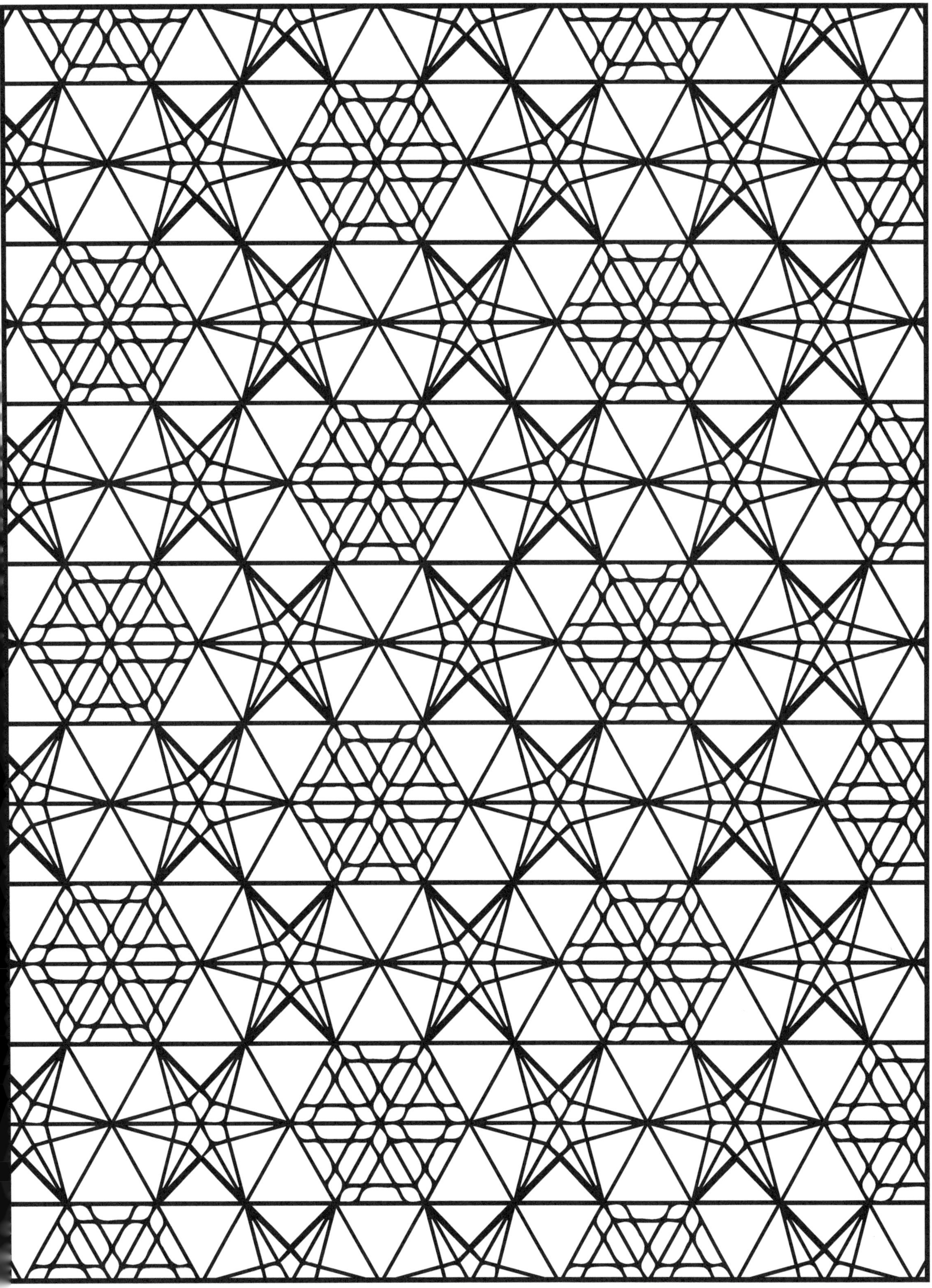

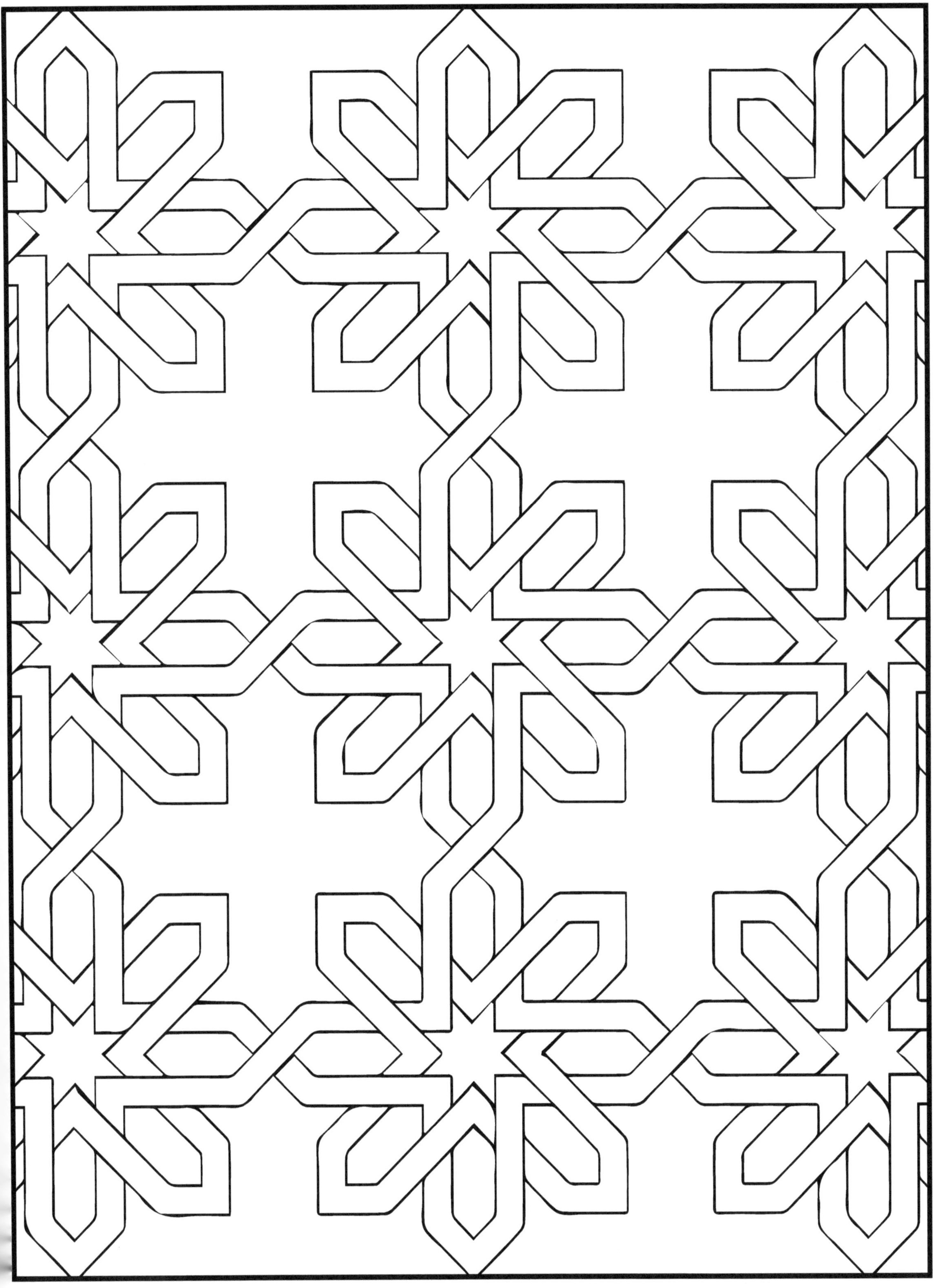

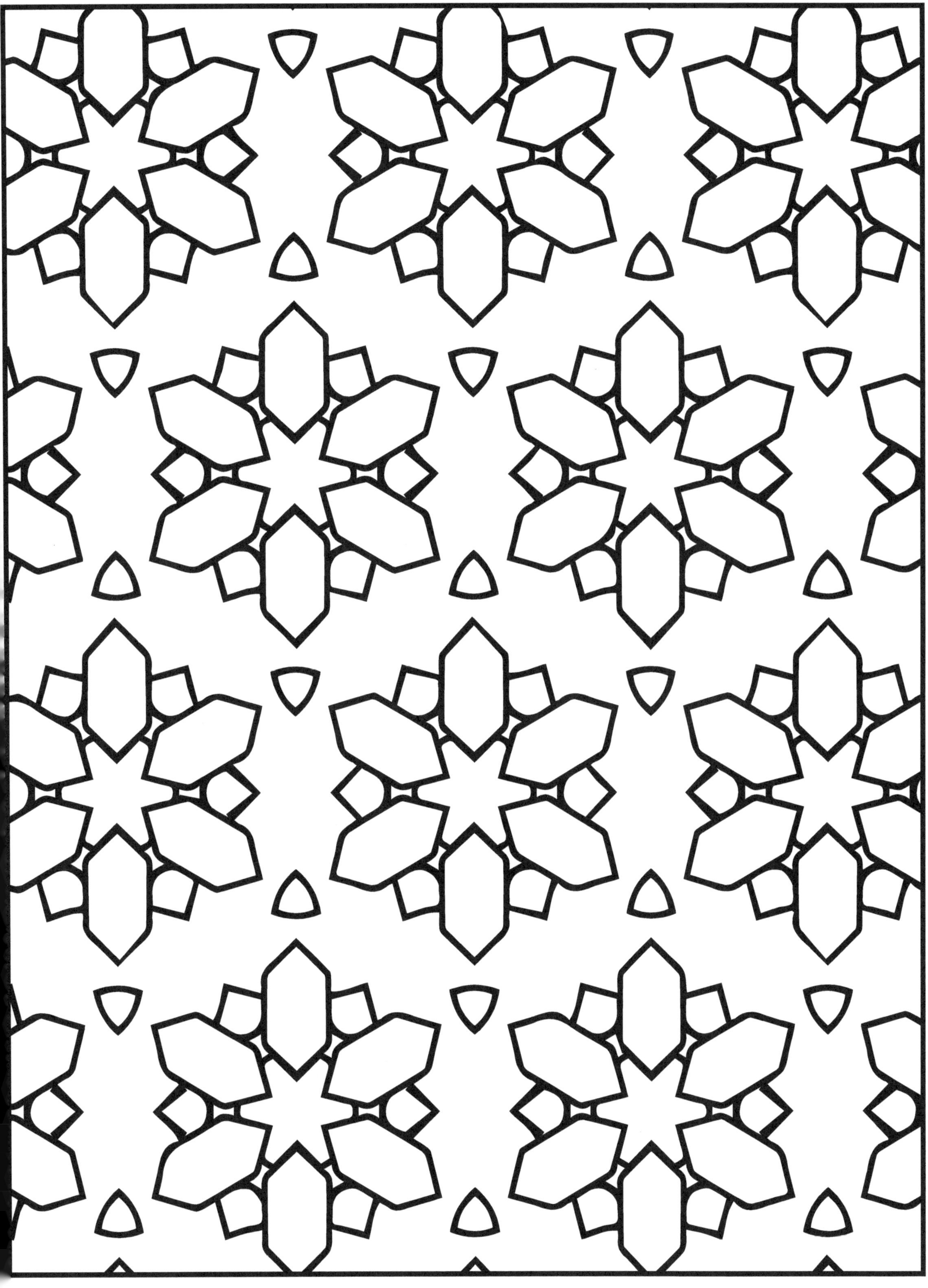

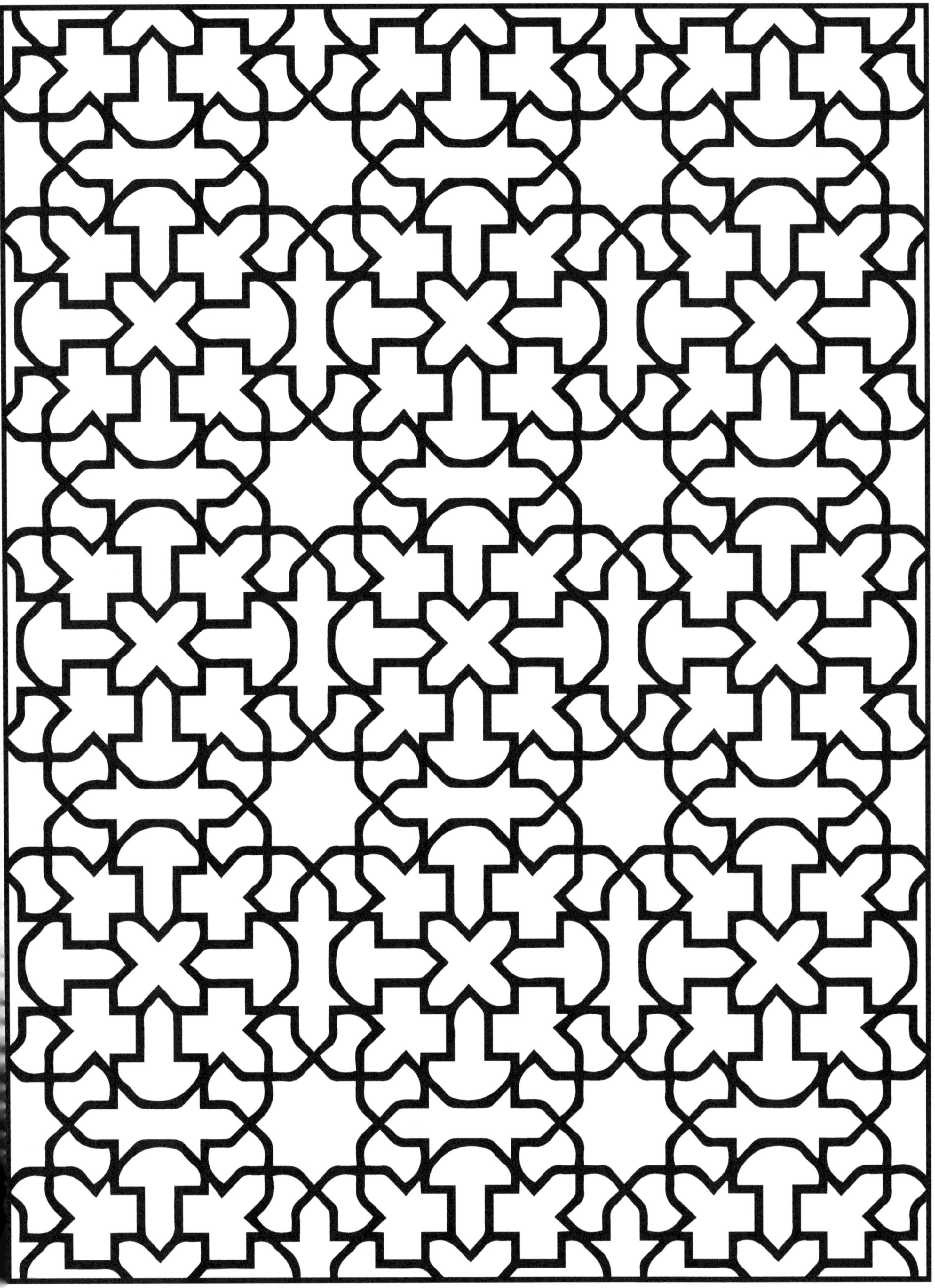

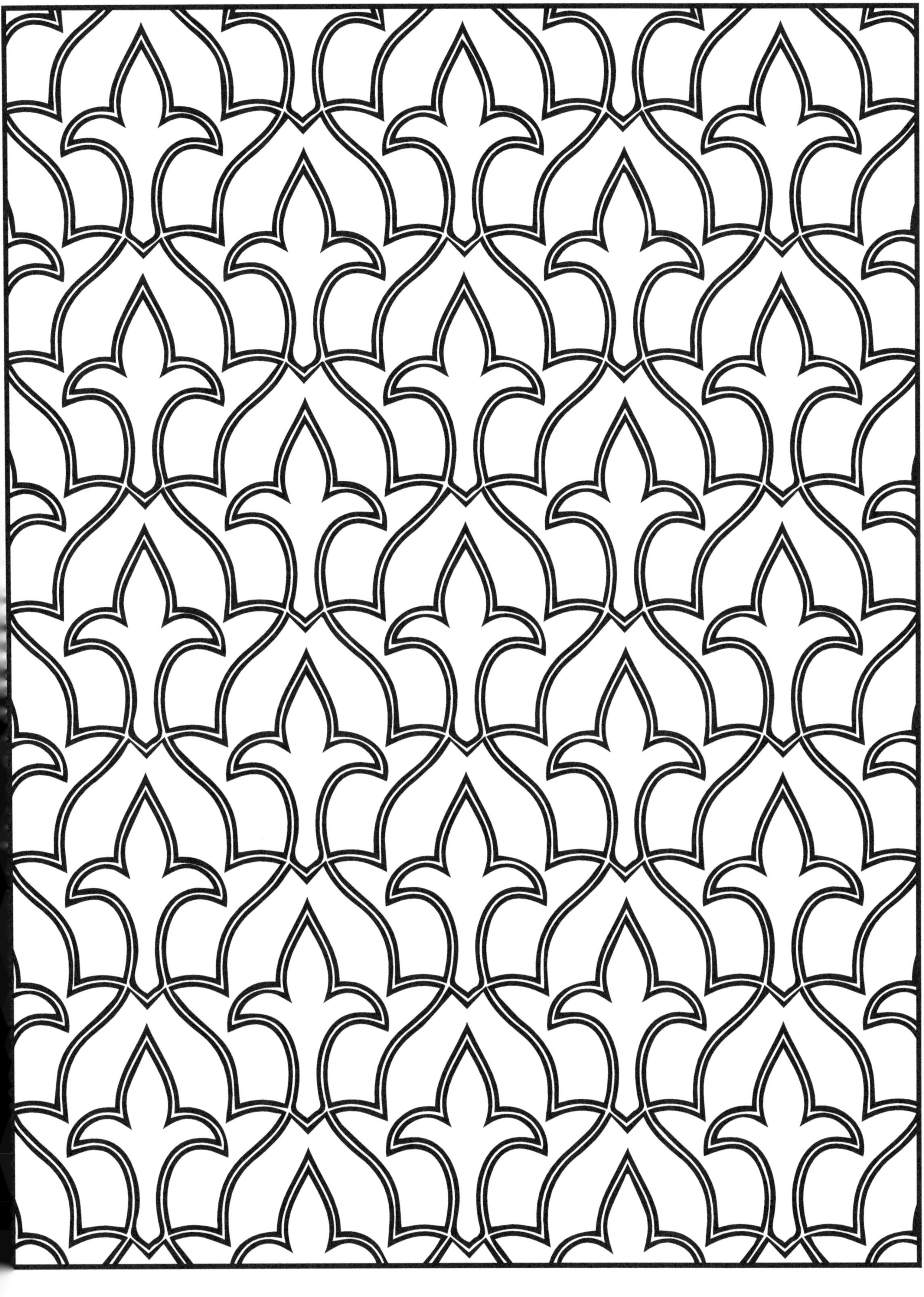

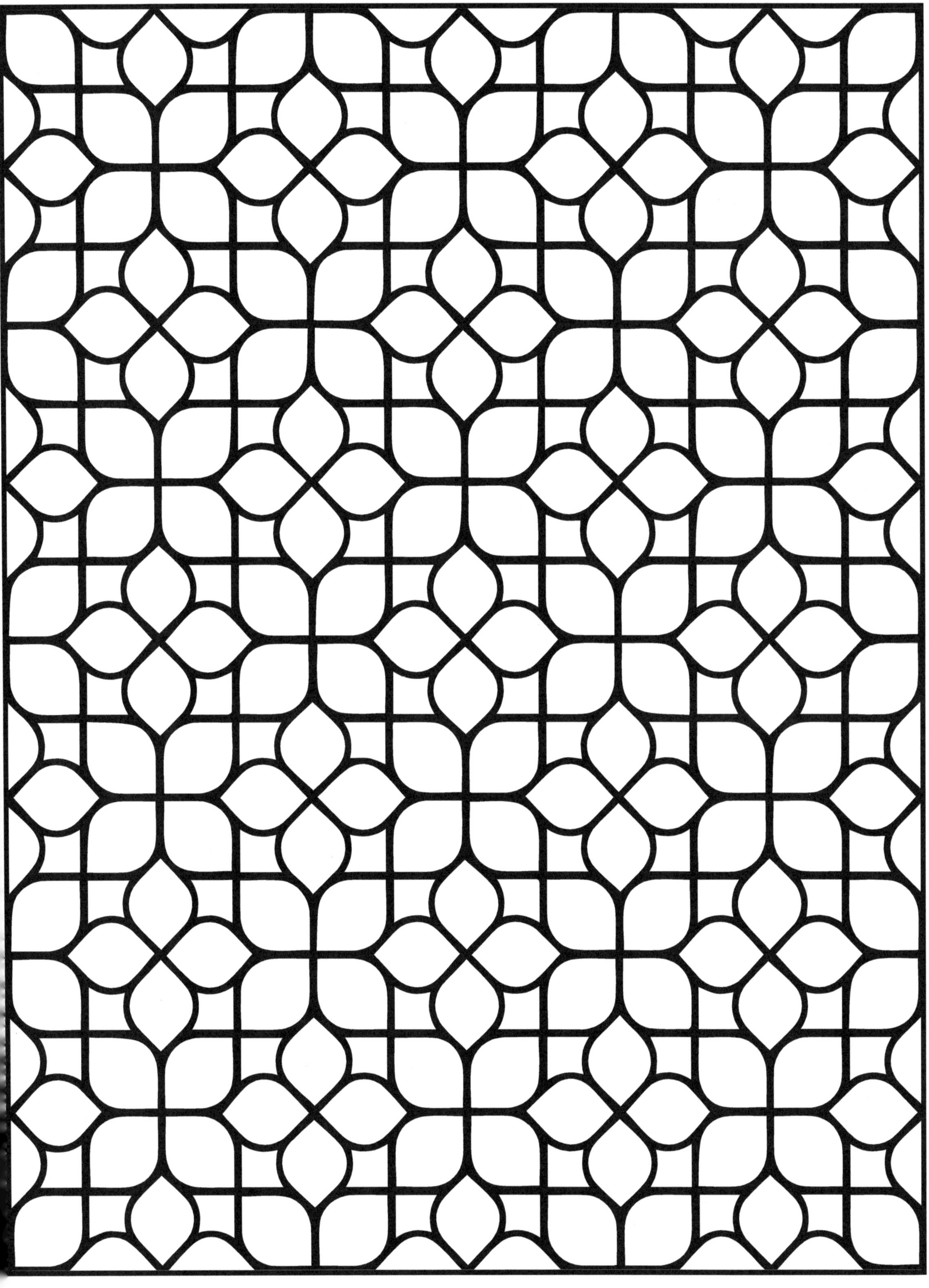

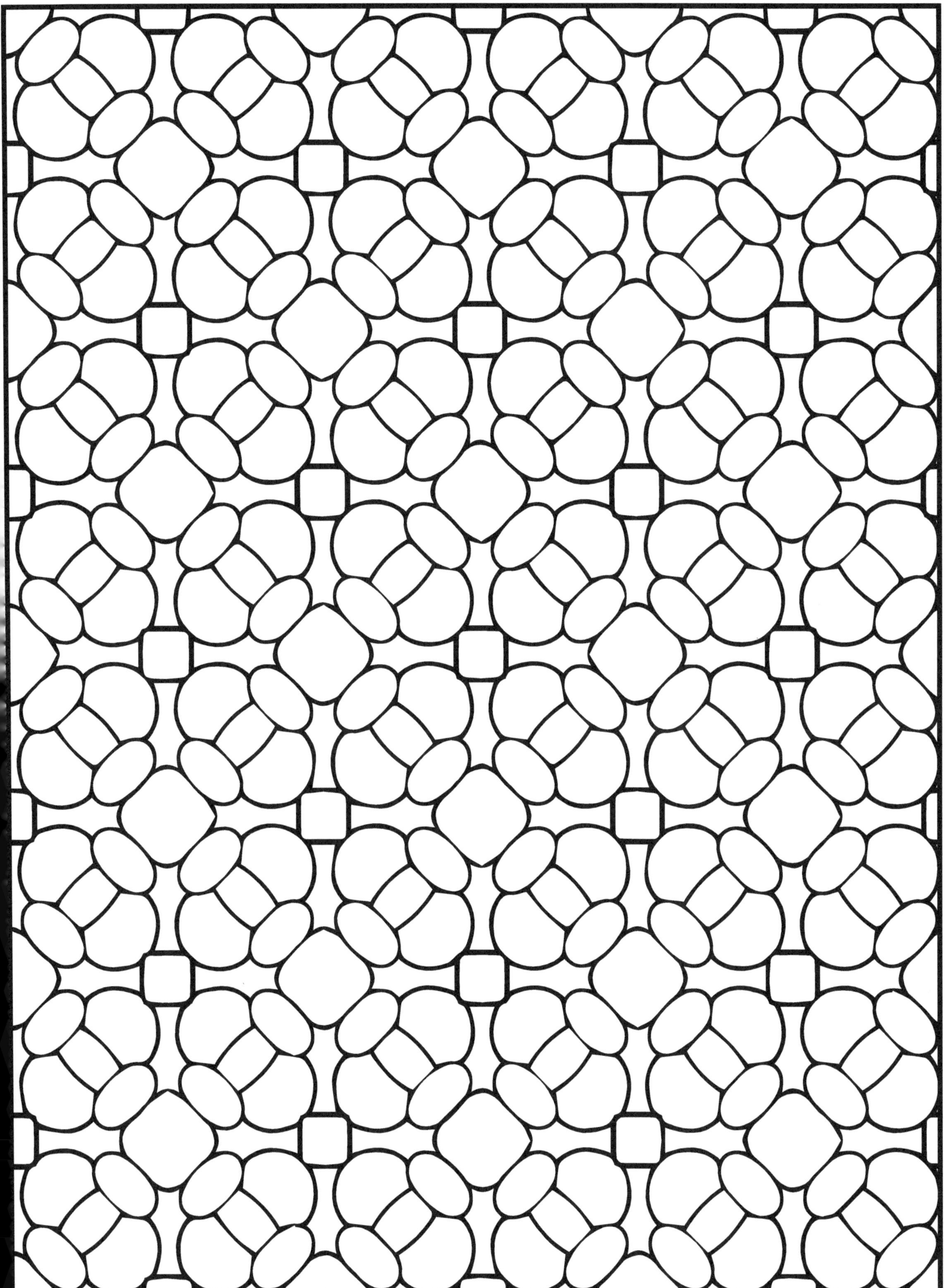

Made in United States
Troutdale, OR
07/07/2023

11032957R00046